Teacher-Centered Schools

Reimagining Education Reform in the Twenty-First Century

Rosetta Marantz Cohen
Samuel Scheer

A SCARECROWEDUCATION BOOK

The Scarecrow Press, Inc.
Lanham, Maryland, and Oxford
2003

A SCARECROWEDUCATION BOOK

Published in the United States of America
by Scarecrow Press, Inc.
A Member of the Rowman & Littlefield Publishing Group
4501 Forbes Blvd., Suite 200, Lanham, MD 20706
www.scarecroweducation.com

PO Box 317
Oxford
OX2 9RU, UK

British Library Cataloguing in Publication Information Available

Library of Congress Cataloging-in-Publication Data

Cohen, Rosetta Marantz.
 Teacher-centered schools : reimagining education reform in the
twenty-first century / Rosetta Marantz Cohen, Samuel Scheer.
   p. cm.
 "A ScarecrowEducation book."
 Includes bibliographical references (p.) and index.
 ISBN 0-8108-4686-1 (pbk. : alk. paper)
  1. Teachers—Job satisfaction—United States.   2. Teacher
effectiveness—United States. 3. School improvement programs—
United States.   I. Scheer, Samuel.   II. Title.
LB2840 .C58   2003
 371.1—dc21   2002153625

♾ ™The paper used in this publication meets the minimum
requirements of American National Standard for Information
Sciences—Permanence of Paper for Printed Library Materials,
ANSI/NISO Z39.48-1992.
Manufactured in the United States of America.

Contents

Acknowledgments   v

Preface   vii

1 Teacher-Centered Schools   1

2 Salaries   15

3 Environment   37

4 Training, Recruitment, and Hiring   59

5 Tenure and School Governance   77

6 A Utopian Vision: Case Study of William Dewey   99

Bibliography   115

Index   122

About the Authors   126

Acknowledgments

We wish to thank our friends and colleagues on the faculty of Smith College and Windsor High School for their ongoing interest and support of this project. We are particularly grateful to Sam Intrator, whose sympathetic input and keen eye for supporting source material was immensely helpful to us. Finally, we are grateful to Thomas Koerner, editorial director at Scarecrow-Education, who recognized from the beginning the value of our ideas.

Preface

In the summer of 2002 an article in the *New York Times* offered uncharacteristically good news about the New York City schools. The paper reported that more than 2,000 certified teachers from all over the country had flocked to a job fair in Brooklyn. What is more, 4,300 openings in the city schools had been filled by mid-July, bringing the system ahead of its usual schedule for hiring. "We're seeing a whole different kind of buzz about . . . teaching in New York City than we've seen before," Randi Weingarten, president of the United Federation of Teachers, told a reporter.[1]

Why the sudden change in a system that has been nationally renowned for its beleaguered status? It is because New York City's mayor, Michael Bloomberg, chose to approach the city's education problem in a new and commonsensical way. These are some of the changes that Bloomberg has implemented since taking office:

1. He has cut administrative bloat in New York City schools by doing away with the infamous Board of Education, wresting control away from that sprawling, inefficient, decentralized bureaucracy and moving the school department into his own building at Tweed Courthouse. Money saved from the reorganization is being pumped back into teacher salaries and maintenance.

2. He has raised teacher salaries from 16 to 22 percent across the board and has raised the maximum starting salary that can be offered to teachers hired from outside the district from $43,370 to $61,000. So far, according to Weingarten,

the higher pay has done far more to attract new teachers than the $8 million advertising campaign the Board of Education ran in previous years.

3. Finally, he has made cosmetic improvements to the work environments of teachers: fixing broken windows and implementing a more efficient system for maintaining school buildings and getting work orders.

Bloomberg, the article goes on to say, has been "quiet" regarding all the usual subjects upon which school reform–minded mayors expound. He has said nothing about bilingual education, math curriculum, or reading scores. Instead, he has focused on concrete economic and structural changes that affect the quality of life of New York City teachers. And it seems to be working.

Bloomberg's logical reforms offer a good test case for the thesis of this book: Change the conditions of teaching, and you change the quality of teachers. Change the quality of teachers, and you change the quality of education. It is simple and obvious, but it has eluded reformers since the start of American public education.

We came to this thesis many years ago. As two teachers, married to each other and living in New York, we spent countless dinner conversations railing at the idiocy of the school bureaucracy, inefficient administrators, standardized tests, and wasteful spending. We lived with the consequences of poor teacher pay and suffered the indignities associated with school disciplinary practices. Later, when our careers took us into higher education, our conversation broadened to include the problems associated with uncertified teachers, the struggles of new teachers in the field, and the uses of good teacher education.

In the late 1980s, when the school restructuring movement was under way, we threw our energies, idealistically, into the notion of an "essential school," a program of creative, interdisciplinary curriculum reform that promised to change the way students thought about their learning. Ultimately, the essential schools movement didn't work any better than any of the dozens of mandates, programs, and curricular initiatives the two of us had witnessed in our careers. And deep down, we always knew why: Every reform we had implemented, whether as teacher or teacher trainer, as reformer or reformee, was always about the kids or the curriculum or the subject matter. It was never about the teacher.

In 1999, we began to lay out in writing the ideas in this book, and we circulated the draft among our friends and colleagues. When people kept asking us for more copies, we knew we were on to something. In 2002, our ideas were published in the educational journal *Phi Delta Kappan*, and the response was again quite remarkable.[2] Teachers from all over the country told us that the article had expressed what they had long been saying to one another in faculty lounges and at dinner parties—basic truths about the profession that rarely make it into print.

It has been a labor of love for us to expand that article into this book. We dedicate it to every great teacher in America, in hopes that a truly teacher-centered school awaits them in the not-so-distant future.

NOTES

1. Anemona Hartocollis, "Levy Says Higher Pay Is Helping to Lure Teachers to New York." *New York Times,* 25 July 2002.

2. Rosetta M. Cohen, "Schools Our Teachers Deserve: A Proposal for Teacher-Centered Schools," *Phi Delta Kappan* 83, no. 7 (March 2002): 532–37.

CHAPTER 1

Teacher-Centered Schools

The title of this book may well have caught the reader off guard. Teacher-centered schools? Why should anyone support such a premise? The notion might seem at first anachronistic, or naïve, or even subversive. Aren't schools supposed to be about children?

For more than five decades now, warehouses full of writing on school reform have focused on the needs of the students—on "learner-centered schools," "student-centered pedagogies," "child-centered classrooms." "Its all about the kids!" intones administrators all over America, and their words echo in every disaffected, demoralized, student-centered high school building in the land. The whole failed history of modern educational reform, from the prescriptive lesson plan formats of the 1970s, to restructuring plans of the 1980s, to the state testing and curriculum frameworks of the 1990s, has addressed "the needs of the child."

It is our contention that the reason why so little changes in American education, why reforms cycle in and out of vogue and problems persist over decades, is because all these theories and policies and mandates fail to adequately address the needs and concerns of *teachers*—the single most fundamental force for educational improvement. "In this school, the teacher comes first." We would wager that there isn't a public school in the land with such a motto. School reform efforts most frequently proceed *despite* teachers, not because of them. John Dewey himself could write a school's curriculum, but if the teachers implementing that curriculum are unhappy or poorly educated or overworked, the quality of instruction will be pedestrian, at best.

Communities can threaten schools all they want to about raising test scores, but if the teachers within those schools are incompetent, if they feel unappreciated and underpaid, nothing will improve over the long term.

For a school to be an intellectual center, for it to have the ethos and the sense of community and the spirit that so many parents and administrators seek, it must celebrate the work of the teacher in a way that is rarely seen in public schools: It must attend to the teacher's needs, the teacher's sensibility, the teacher's contribution, with as much genuine concern as it does any other constituency—and maybe more. While school reformers think in terms of what should be taught, how, with what materials, an honest teacher will tell you that *the teacher* is more important than the curriculum. His or her attitude, affect, and persona have more impact on student learning than does the book used or the pedagogic technique employed. One need only think back on one's own best teachers to know how true this is: The text and the technique have long been forgotten; the teacher is remembered—the human being, the passion, intelligence, and energy.

The fact that no book has yet been written on this subject is in itself, we believe, a testament to our thesis. Presidents and policy makers search for solutions to America's educational ills in every place but the obvious one. Again and again, the problem is defined in terms of test scores and literacy levels, parent involvement, student self-esteem, drugs and violence. For all their inflamed rhetoric about an "educational crisis," neither Clinton nor Bush ever once made substantive recommendations concerning the status and conditions of *teaching*.

There is an educational crisis in America, but it is not the crisis about which our political leaders speak. The crisis is in the quality of America's teaching force, both now and in the near future. If demographers are to be believed, we are poised on the brink of an unprecedented teacher shortage. Over 50 percent of America's teachers are currently over forty-five years of age. If these individuals retire at predicted rates, we will need to hire over two million new teachers by the year 2007.[1] Given the state of the field, given public attitudes toward teaching and the conditions under which many teachers work, we will never be able to find enough good teachers to fill those positions. Our schools, it seems, are destined to be filled with even greater numbers of poorly trained and uninspired individuals.

In the past, when America has been confronted with a true crisis, we have spared no expense in resolving it. We spend billions of dollars on Star Wars defense systems to defend America against some imagined future attack. The "crisis" that emerged with our savings and loan industry was met almost at once with seemingly limitless federal money. But ironically, it is often precisely at those moments when rhetoric about education is most heated that teacher salaries and teacher prestige fall to their lowest point. When Reagan called America "a nation at risk," the reforms he sponsored ultimately served to undermine the appeal of the teaching profession rather than to elevate it.² Similarly, we rail today about falling test scores, and yet conditions for teachers in many schools are worse than they were ten years ago. Nationally, teachers' relative standard of living is the lowest it has been in forty years, and the average teacher salary increase in the year 2000 was smaller than it has been in two generations![3] Where is the federal commitment to our educational defense? Where are the billions for teacher salaries and school construction?

Study after study tells us that student achievement is directly correlated to the quality of American teachers.⁴ When teachers are good, test scores go up, attrition rates go down, and parents express confidence in their public schools. If we restructure schools to make teaching appealing to talented people, reform education to attract and retain the best and brightest, we will have gone a long way toward resolving America's "education crisis."

WHERE ARE ALL THE GREAT TEACHERS?

This book addresses the current teacher crisis as a two-part problem: how to attract the brightest young people into the field and then how to keep them. What incentives can we offer to attract and maintain a talented and committed work force?

To attract the talented college graduate, America must come to terms with a cultural reality: Most smart young people don't become teachers anymore. Until the 1970s, American communities were in the privileged position of having a ready-made pool of talent to staff their schools. With career options drastically circumscribed, educated women historically chose teaching as the one viable profession available to them. Since the 1980s, the numbers of top women entering the teaching force has fallen off dramatically, not only because of their access to other careers, but also because of the profession's association with an "unenlightened" past. Where once, on national surveys, the vast majority of female college graduates cited teaching as their preferred occupation, now only a tiny percentage will even consider it.[5]

The same retreat from teaching has occurred, of course, among highly talented men. For a brief time, during the late 1960s and early 1970s, such men were entering the teaching field in numbers that seemed to reverse historical precedent. Draft-avoiders and idealists, these activist young people are largely responsible for the modest improvements in teachers' working conditions and salaries that occurred in the late 1960s and early 1970s. This period of activism brought to light serious inequities and opened the way to a new kind of public advocacy for urban schools. But, by the mid-1980s, the new generation of this cohort had all but abandoned the profession for higher-profile occupations or more prestigious kinds of service work, leaving schools to scramble for any warm body they could corral into the classroom. Teaching simply did not provide a powerful enough lure to maintain the interest of the post-Vietnam generation.

The retreat from teaching by America's best and brightest is not, we believe, an inevitable sociological phenomenon. Even today, in the best colleges around the country, enrollments in introductory education classes are often extremely high. Talented students *are* initially curious about the profession; idealistic students *are* still willing to consider it as a career. But many of these students are chased away from the profession even before they have had a chance to begin: Too often, assigned readings in education classes are banal or infantile—pitched to the least intellectual cohort in the institution. Students quickly glean that the work of teachers is scripted and controlled. What is more, when students do observations and internships in local schools, they are often put off by what they see there—the drudgery, the heavy workloads, the cynicism of the institution and its inhabitants. These factors must be changed if good people are even to consider teaching as a career.

Retaining good teachers and keeping veteran teachers energized is an even more challenging problem for schools. Recently, we sat in a crowd of perhaps three thousand educators at the keynote address of the American Educational Research Association's annual conference. Around us were academics from every state in the U.S., professors of education, and graduate students, who had come to present, in their allotted fifteen or twenty minutes, a sliver of research over which they had no doubt labored for many months. More than half of these academics, we reckoned, must have started their careers as classroom teachers. That's the standard route for professors of education. What happened? Why did so many intelligent people leave a profession they had once chosen? Was it really so much more satisfying for those thousands of individuals to write their monographs on cooperative learning than it would have been to impact the lives of America's schoolchildren? Certainly, salaries had not been the key factor in their leaving the field; everyone knows that college salaries are often no better than public school salaries. Workload was probably not the deciding factor either: Entry-level assistant professors work every bit as hard as schoolteachers do; their classes are often enormous, and the pressures to publish complicate the lives of young academics.

Clearly, then, it was probably something in the conditions of school teaching that drove many of these intelligent people away. Perhaps it was their perceived lack of prestige in the community, or the absence of intellectual collegiality within their schools; perhaps it was their lack of creative discretion over the curriculum, or inadequate administrative support, or the demeaning ancillary responsibilities—the cafeteria duties and study halls. Maybe a threat of violence drove the best away, or the realization that hard work goes routinely unrewarded and unpraised in public schools. The reasons for teacher attrition are rarely explored and discussed. Schools just shrug their shoulders and let teachers go, scrambling in July and August for new hires to fill the places of those who have left.

As for those who do stay on—the veteran teachers of America —is it any wonder so many are victims of burnout? Working under adverse conditions over time, with good colleagues leaving around you and a culture of dissatisfaction pervading your work environment, even the most robust spirit would be tested. As any high school student will avow, the sullenness and exhaustion of these individuals, their cynicism and contempt for the system, are a potent disincentive to student learning. Compared to teacher morale, poorly written curricula and scheduling and structural concerns are of such small importance that they might as well not be factors at all.

But schools can reform in ways that would decrease both attrition and burnout among veteran teachers. Changes can be made in the structure of schools, in their civil norms, and in their distribution of power that would have real and lasting effects on the teaching force—retaining some who would otherwise leave, and energizing some who would otherwise become "dead wood," an immovable burden on the system.

A HISTORY OF INVISIBILITY

Redefining the teaching profession—reimagining it as important and prestigious work—means coming to terms with the profession's bleak history and with the stereotypes that dog the field. Many Americans still think of teachers as failed adults, those who could not engage successfully with the world. It is assumed that those with audacious, adventurous spirits or with keen intellects do not become teachers. These assumptions go back almost to the founding of our country, and they will not be easily overturned. Even our most proeducation president, Thomas Jefferson, recommended in his 1789 Bill for the More General Diffusion of

Knowledge, that those students who failed to make the cut for William and Mary—that is, those who were not bright enough to qualify for college scholarships—be made the teachers of the young.

A teacher holds sway over children, an essentially suspect circumstance. One finds evidence of this bias in America's earliest literature, in the depiction of Ichabod Crane by Washington Irving and in the works of John Trumbull and Philip Freneau.[6] These early republican writers reflected in their satires on teaching the American prejudice against working with children. Teachers like Ichabod Crane were portrayed as unmanly and effete. Readers in the eighteenth century, most of whom had struggled to build farms and work the land, must have been pleased to have an object of easy ridicule—a man (in those days teachers were almost always men) who chose to spend his day in the schoolroom.

To make matters worse, high school teachers in America were essentially teachers of Latin and Greek—dead languages that seemed (and were) as useless to the rugged pioneer laborers of America as any subject could be. Indeed, even the usefulness of basic literacy was suspect to many farmers. It's no wonder children misbehaved so outrageously in early American schools. They brought with them, no doubt, all the overt and implied contempt of their parents for the profession of teaching and the work of the school. And the solution to that misbehavior simply served to exacerbate the problem: The tradition of corporal punishment helped to cast teachers, in the public imagination, as bullies and cowards—a role that seems to hang over the teacher to this day.

Nor was the American stereotype of the teacher helped by the feminization of the profession in the early nineteenth century. At that point, when a population explosion created an unprecedented demand for educators, America found that its tendency to degrade the profession left few men willing to take up the work. By default, women entered the field. They were lured by a calculated campaign, led by common school reformers like Horace Mann and James Carter, which cast the profession of teaching in spiritual terms. Instructing children was "God's work," and teaching would serve to fulfill and complete a woman's natural gifts—her pious and self-sacrificing nature.

What is more, women could teach before marriage as a kind of dry run for domestic life. Through sacrifice and service to the community, the argument went, women would become ideal wives and mothers. At this point many other stubborn stereotypes got their start: "She's a born teacher" means she is nurturing and sympathetic, patient and pliant—teacher as martyr. Women lack natural ambition, wrote Horace Mann, they seek no honors from the world: This makes them ideal teachers.[7]

The explosion of public schools in the mid-nineteenth century, along with new laws regarding compulsory education, was a pivotal moment in the life of the profession. Economist Susan Carter has noted that if teachers of the period had understood how badly they were needed, how dire the crisis really was, they would have had the leverage to command much more respectable wages.[8] Instead, the women who followed Mann's evangelical call accepted the paltriest salaries imaginable, thereby setting the precedent for two centuries of low pay. Today, when bond issues fail to pass and teachers' salaries remain low, many justify the situation by echoing those common school reformers: "You shouldn't be teaching for the money. You should be teaching for the spiritual satisfaction."

From the mid-nineteenth century on, the treatment of teachers in many respects mirrors the treatment of American women in general: By the 1850s, especially in urban areas, teachers were essentially stripped of all decision-making power, any discretion over curriculum, and even the capacity to make minor pedagogical choices. Following the model of industry, schools restructured themselves to become educational factories, where male administrators wielded absolute power over female teacher-workers, controlling and harassing them in ways that were sometimes Dickensian in their cruelty. Scientific managers created rigid rules for classroom teachers. There was one way to ask a question, one way to hold a book.[9] The era gave rise to teachers' unions, organizations formed by women in a feeble attempt to defend themselves against a hostile society. Teachers, of course, could not marry, and, until the unions succeeded in creating a pension system, retired teachers survived at the mercy of their colleagues, who would "pass around the hat" to support them.[10]

Once teachers began to fight for their rights through unions, a whole new series of stereotypes began to dog them. Sociologist Dan Lortie writes that although nineteenth-century teachers had been poor and powerless, they retained a kind of psychological power in their communities—what Lortie calls a "ritual pity."[11] They were admired, as one might admire nuns, for their sacrifices (of husbands and children, of money and prestige), even as they were refused decent compensation. Once teachers started fighting for their rights, however, they became mercenary and hard in the public imagination. When they went still further and insti tuted strikes in the 1960s—often for things as basic as a lunch break or a $200 raise—they lost even more support in their communities. Teachers were no longer saints and martyrs but (once again) blue-collar workers. Union activity in the 1960s seemed to strip all romance and cachet from the profession.

Today, American teachers seem to embody, in the public imagination, all of their complex history at once. The recent spate of school shootings rekindled in the media a vision of the teacher as martyr, struggling to correct the social ills of the society. The faltering economy renewed the complaint that teachers are over paid and lazy, their long summer vacations and abbreviated work hours a testament to the ease of the work.

These persistent and contradictory stereotypes of the teacher—as self-sacrificing and mercenary, self-abnegating and lazy—seem uniquely American. It is curious that, while America compares its educational system with those of Japan and Western Europe, we persistently fail to compare the image and treatment of teachers in these countries. No developed country in Europe or Asia holds the kinds of stereotypes of teachers that we do. In France, Spain, and Germany teachers enjoy a high status. Teaching carries enormous prestige in Japanese culture, where teachers are called *sensei,* an honorific term of respect. It is not unusual to see business and civic leaders bowing to their former schoolteachers.[12] According to the U.S. Department of Education, competition for teaching jobs in Japan is fierce on both the high school and elementary school levels. In Naka City schools, for example, there are thirty-five highly qualified applicants for every social studies job, ten for every math job, and nine for every science position. The competition for jobs among elementary schoolteachers is comparably stiff.[13] It is not unusual for a talented young person in Japan to enroll in law school or business school only after failing to secure a position as a high school teacher. Given such attitudes toward teaching, is it any wonder that Japanese students are well-behaved and studious? It is not only that an ethos of achievement is embedded in the Japanese culture, it is also that teachers are worthy of respect; their work is valued and their profession is revered.

While we don't imagine that America could so transform its norms and values that our teachers would receive the respect given to their Japanese counterparts, some of that distance can be bridged. Changes can be made in the profession; policies can force a shift of attitudes. For the sake of America's future, it must happen.

In the chapters that follow, we describe those reforms. We begin, in the next chapter, with the subject of compensation. What is a fair wage for the work we ask of teachers? How can budgets be allocated to put funding where it will do the most good? We consider at some length the problem of administrative bloat—the misuse of tax revenues for central office personnel and other expendable bureaucrats at the expense of teacher wages. Understanding that salaries for jobs in the public sector are necessarily circumscribed, we then look at other forms of compensation, to be borne by federal and state governments, that might supplement wages and entice good candidates into the field. We call for more portable pensions, for housing and tax incentives, and for other forms of support that would place little burden on the individual citizen.

Chapter 3 deals with the teacher's work environment. It considers the problem of discipline—the factor that, more than any other, drives good teachers out of the field. We look at the ways in which student behavior is addressed, and to whom that responsibility is delegated. We call for major reforms in this area, including reforms in legislation that protects chronically disruptive students and legislation regarding the rights of teachers to act on their own behalf. In chapter 3 we also discuss physical structures of schools, their cafeterias and lavatories, and how the environment often undercuts the work of the teacher—and by extension the quality of the students' academic experience.

Chapter 4 looks at the key issues of training, recruitment, and hiring. We begin by considering the growing movement for alternative certification and the systematic attack, in recent years, on teacher education. We believe that the motives behind the dismantling of teacher training are suspect, and we argue in defense of excellent, well-funded teacher education. We then examine the process of hiring, arguably the most important work of any school administration. We describe the often slipshod hiring practices that currently exist in schools and present proposals for improving that process—through extensive teacher involvement and through more active, aggressive recruiting. Finally, we consider the ways in which new teachers are (and are not) socialized into the profession.

We look at other professions as models for better recruitment and for strategies for mentoring talented young teachers instead of throwing them into untenable work environments and expecting them to "rise to the challenge." We discuss ways to retain the best teachers—looking to colleges, private schools, and corporations for models of meaningful incentives. These include the creation of sabbaticals and changes in the nature of teachers' duties (America's best and brightest should not be monitoring bathrooms during their free periods). Finally, we examine the proper role of the administration in stemming teacher attrition.

Chapter 5, "Tenure and School Governance," first considers the problems of evaluation. Improving American education will require the profession to engage in serious self-scrutiny; to ask the question many teachers resist: Why are so many poor and incompetent teachers allowed to remain in the field? If we are to reform the profession, if we are to dignify it with better salaries and working conditions and raise its status in the culture, teachers will have to police themselves in ways that many have been unwilling to do in the past.

We discuss tests and strategies to determine whether a teacher is good enough to remain in a position and how the tenure system might be revised to become a truly useful mechanism for teacher evaluation. Next, the chapter considers the ways in which schools are currently governed. We suggest a model that avoids wasteful spending and utilizes the expertise of teachers—those who are closest to the pulse of the school and best understand issues of mentoring, professional development, and hiring and firing.

Chapter 5 also addresses curriculum design, school governance, and professional development from the perspective of the teacher, a perspective too rarely addressed in the literature. Decisions about what should be taught and how are routinely made without input from anyone charged with implementing those decisions. Too many teachers today, like those in the nineteenth century, wait "down on the factory floor" while their bosses, in the district's central office or at the state department of education, debate what texts to use, what tests to administer, or what pedagogy to follow. Likewise, we discuss professional development, or in-service instruction, another area that would benefit from teacher input.

Finally, in chapter 6, we offer a case study of a teacher-centered school and describe how it would be to teach in such a place. It may be an ideal vision of a teacher's work, but it is not out of reach. The point of this book is that meaningful change is possible. Though teaching will probably never be able to compete on a salary level with other prestigious professions, we believe that certain small, key changes in the culture of teaching would make the profession attractive to young people. If only one percent of the top five percent of American college students chose to teach, it would have a remarkably salutary effect. Transform American schools into teacher-centered institutions—adult-friendly places where teachers are made to feel like valued pro-

fcssionals—and you will be helping students in the most fundamental, lasting, and meaningful way.

NOTES

1. Linda Darling-Hammond, *What Matters Most: Teaching for
America's Future* (New York: National Commission on Teaching and
America's Future, 1996).

2. U.S. Department of Education, *Digest of Education Statistics*
(Washington, D.C., 1999), http://nces.ed.gov/pubs2000/digest99/. Federal funding for elementary and secondary education programs fell 22
percent between 1975 and 1980.

3. American Federation of Teachers, AFL-CIO, *Survey & Analysis
of Teacher Salary Trends 2000*, http://www.aft.org/research. See figs.
1-5 and 1-6.

4. Insofar as there are links between teacher characteristics and
classroom effectiveness, the strongest of these involve verbal ability.
This has been known since the famed Coleman report of 1966, when
teacher scores on a verbal test were the only school input found to have
a positive relationship to student achievement. See Christopher S. Jencks, "The Coleman Report and the Conventional Wisdom," in *On
Equality of Educational Opportunity*, eds. Frederick Mosteller and Daniel Patrick Moynihan (New York: Random House, 1972), 69–115. See
also Ronald F. Ferguson, "Can Schools Narrow the Black-White Test
Score Gap," in *The Black-White Test Score Gap*, eds. Christopher Jencks and Meredith Phillips (Washington, D.C.: Brookings Institution
Press, 1998), 318–74. In an analysis of 900 Texas school districts, Ferguson found that teachers' expertise as measured by scores on licensing
examinations accounted for about 40 percent of the measured variance
in students' reading and mathematics achievement at grades 1 through
11, more than any other single factor. He also found that every additional dollar spent on more qualified teachers netted greater increases in
student achievement than did less instructionally focused uses of school
resources. See also Linda Darling-Hammond, "Teacher Quality and
Student Achievement: A Review of State Policy Evidence," *Education
Policy Analysis Archives* 8 (January 2000), http://epaa.asu.edu/epaa/
v8n1/. Darling-Hammond's study concludes: "While student demo-
graphic characteristics are strongly related to student outcomes at the

state level, they are less influential in predicting achievement levels than variables assessing the quality of the teaching force" (p. 36).

5. See William Johnson, "Teachers and Teacher Training in the Twentieth Century," in *American Teachers: Histories of a Profession at Work*, ed. Donald Warren (New York : Macmillan, 1989), 237–56.

6. See John Trumbull, "The Rare Adventures of Tom Brainless," Philip Freneau, "The Private Tutor," and Washington Irving, "The Legend of Sleepy Hollow," in *The Work of Teachers in America: A Social History through Stories,* eds. Rosetta Cohen and Samuel Scheer (Mahwah, N.J.: Lawrence Erlbaum, 1997), 13–35.

7. Horace Mann, *Annual Report of the Board of Education, Together with the Annual Reports of the Secretary of the Board, 1847– 1852* (Washington, D.C.: National Education Association, 1947–1952).

8. See Susan Carter, "Incentives and Rewards to Teaching," in *American Teachers: Histories of a Profession at Work*, ed. Donald Warren (New York: Macmillan, 1989), 49–62.

9. Nancy Hoffman, *Woman's True Profession* (Old Westbury, N.Y.: Feminist Press, 1981). The book offers firsthand accounts of female teachers terrorized by male administrators in urban classrooms at the turn of the twentieth century.

10. Ibid., 200–300. Hoffman's social history of the teaching profession documents the conditions that gave rise to union demands.

11. Dan Lortie, *School Teacher: A Sociological Study* (Chicago: University of Chicago Press, 1977), 1–24.

12. In 2000, we observed this social practice during the semester we taught at Doshisha University in Kyoto. For a scholarly discussion of the status and working conditions of teachers in Japan, see Kaori Okana and Montonori Tsuchiya, *Education in Contemporary Japan: Inequality and Diversity* (Singapore: Cambridge University Press, 1999), 151–85.

13. U.S. Department of Education, *The Educational System in Japan: Case Study Findings 1998* (Washington, D.C., June 1998), http://www.ed.gov/pubs/JapanCaseStudy/. See especially chapter 5.

CHAPTER 2

Salaries

One cannot begin to talk seriously about reforming America's schools without addressing the issues of teacher compensation. Even taking altruism and youthful idealism into account, few talented college graduates will choose to enter a profession that is grossly underpaid, and even fewer remain in that profession over time.[1] Low pay is one of the main reasons why it is so difficult to attract talented people into the profession, and salaries continue to be a central source of teacher dissatisfaction in national polls and surveys.[2] If good teachers make good schools, teacher compensation is the starting point for all meaningful reform.

Teachers are civil servants, and, as such, they will never be able to command the kinds of salaries enjoyed by many specialists in the private sector. Few communities will ever be able to afford $100,000 teachers, the figure recently set forth as a fair wage in a well-publicized critique of the profession.[3] Even Albert Shanker, former president of the American Federation of Teachers, acknowledged that teacher salaries will always be less than those of top professionals in business and industry, and that this is a reality even the union can accept. As Shanker notes, were schools to suddenly raise base pay for top college graduates to levels that competed with the best corporate and law firms, those firms would simply raise salaries again, to draw young talent back into their ranks.[4] Public education would never win a bidding war with the private sector.

But public education cannot and will not improve as long as teachers are paid substandard wages. Teachers should be able to afford the comfort of a middle-class life and have the sense that their labor is valued in real terms by the community. In too many states, this is not the case. Average teacher salaries in the U.S. are poor and getting poorer. In 1994, teachers earned, nationwide, an average of $11,000 less than other college graduates. Just four years later, in 1998, the gap had grown to over $18,000. For workers with master's degrees, the salary differential is even more dramatic: In 1994, the gap between teachers and nonteachers was almost $13,000; by 1998 it had widened to more than $25,000. Young teachers, ages 22 to 28, began their careers, in 1998, with an average salary of only $21,792. Nonteachers with bachelor's degrees averaged $30,000 to start.[5]

Teacher salaries look particularly meager when viewed over decades: Over the course of the 1980s, when the American economy was booming, the median starting salaries for teachers actually lost ground—both in real terms and relative to most other professional and semiprofessional fields. According to the 1999 census data, teacher salaries increased a mere 19 percent between 1980 and 1997. During the same period, salaries overall in the U.S. increased by 29 percent. Between 1991 and 2001, average teachers' salaries, adjusted for inflation, grew a mere 0.3 percent per year. Since consumer prices rose an average of 2.5 percent per year over the same period, teachers actually lost out against inflation, and substantially so.[6]

A BRIEF HISTORY OF TEACHER COMPENSATION

How is it that teachers have come to be so poorly paid? Why is it that their salaries are often the last demand that communities are willing to meet when negotiating reforms in their schools?

Like so many other aspects of the profession, teacher salaries reflect, in quite explicit ways, the attitudes and prejudices that were formed earlier in our history. The previous chapter presented an overview of historical factors that contributed to the low status of teachers in America: the entrenched anti-intellectualism and the biases associated with a feminized profession. Low pay and poor compensation are certainly tied to those entrenched stereotypes.

America's earliest teachers were itinerants who worked only several months of the year, in hope of scraping together sufficient money to move west or start a business. Though early schools were "community-financed" by law, towns were under no obligation to support the schools in any but the most meager fashion.[7] In the eighteenth and early nineteenth centuries teachers were paid largely by "rate bills," a system that allowed a family to be charged per child for the number of days that child attended school. Rate bills created chronic, parent-sanctioned absenteeism on the part of students and are generally seen as the source of much early animosity toward the teacher. Teachers were held accountable for student learning and behavior to an almost absurd degree. It was easy to withhold rate bill payments, and many parents found ways to pay as seldom and as little as possible.

By the early nineteenth century, rate bills had been nearly abolished in public schools, but compensation was still meagre at best. Until late in the century, most female teachers were paid through what was essentially a barter system. Teachers "boarded round," living in the homes of their students. Room and board was then subtracted from the teacher's wages, leaving almost nothing in terms of cash salary. What is more, communities tended to share the burden of housing the teacher by moving her from family to family, with little advance notice. There are countless tales of teachers exploited in these homes— conscripted to work as full-time babysitters, nurses, and domestics—all the while being reminded that their status in the house was provisional and based on the charitable largesse of the homeowner. Teachers' journals and letters bear testimony to other forms of abuse: For example, communities would contract to pay their teacher once a year, and then claim, at the end of the term, that the students did not show sufficient academic improvement to warrant any payment at all.[8]

The move to regularize common schools at the end of the nineteenth century finally formalized pay structures. In many communities, the boarding round system was replaced by a contract-driven pay scale, based on experience and level (elementary or secondary). But compensation still reflected community biases regarding the desirability of the candidate: Men were paid more than women; whites were paid more than blacks.

The feminization of the profession, beginning in the 1830s and peaking at the beginning of the twentieth century, established a precedent of low wages. Teaching had been effectively transformed in the public imagination into a kind of monastic calling, wherein the spiritual uplift of its practitioners was adequate compensation for their labor. This vision of the teacher as "above" pecuniary concerns persisted long into the twentieth century. Teacher contracts from rural schools in the 1930s and 1940s reveal the degree to which young teachers were "kept" by their communities as spiritual servants—or even slaves. A contract from a southern town in 1932 required the teacher to take an oath, pledging to "sleep eight hours a night" and "not to fall in love." The oath ended with the following statement:

> I promise to remember that I owe a duty to the townspeople who are paying me my wages, that I owe respect to the school board and the superintendent that hired me, and that I shall consider myself at all times the willing servant of the school board and the townspeople.[9]

It is not until the rise of the unions that the present single salary schedule was fully adopted. Early union activity brought pensions and improved working conditions and questioned the fairness of a number of common practices in the area of compensation. By the middle of the twentieth century, unions had achieved pay equity for teachers across school level (elementary and secondary teachers were now paid on the same scale) and, at least overtly, across race and gender. Today, the structure of compensation established in the 1960s remains in place: Salaries are established on the district level. Teachers are paid on a fixed scale, according to their years of experience and their advanced degrees. They may also receive additional compensation for ancillary duties, such as coaching, advising clubs, or coordinating after-school activities.

Despite the formalization of the pay schedule, the fixed scale, and ancillary compensation, some aspects of teacher compensation today still hark back to the past. For instance, salaries are still "front-loaded," so cost-of-living increases decrease in size as teachers move up the pay scale. Front-loading accounts for the small change that occurs in wages over the course of a career—a disincentive for teachers to remain in the profession.

The front-loading of pay can be traced to the idiosyncratic nature of the profession early in the twentieth century. Until the 1970s, when men entered the field in larger numbers than previously, female teachers tended to come and go from the classroom in what has been termed a "revolving door" syndrome. Young teachers would teach until marriage, then leave to raise their children. Many years later, they would return to pick up where they left off. Savvy administrators surmised that returning teachers would feel at a disadvantage if their salaries were substantially less than those of unmarried teachers who had remained over time. The result was the front-loading of salaries.

Another carryover from the past that affects compensation today is the nonportability of pensions. At present, teachers who move from one state to another before being vested in a pension plan lose all the money the state has contributed on their behalf over the years of their employment. They can recover the small contributions they themselves have made, but these are minimal compared to the fully funded pensions of colleagues who remain in the same state over a career. Transferring teachers must essentially start their pensions from scratch in the new state.[10] Since pension benefits represent one of the few real perks for teachers, this almost universally applied clause in contracts is burdensome indeed.

The tradition of nonportable pensions also harks back to an earlier period. When pension benefits became standard in compensation packages, teachers were mostly female, unmarried, and immobile; they spent their careers in the communities where they had grown up. Later, once teachers were allowed to marry, their salaries were so small and their career longevity was so brief that few worried about losing money if they left the state to follow a husband. Even as social norms changed, this aspect of the teachers' contract remained fixed.

Finally, one could argue that the whole movement for compensation based on performance is yet another carryover from the past, a modern-day equivalent of the rate bill. The recent attempts to dismantle the single-salary schedule seem to be inspired, at times, by the same parsimony and suspicion that characterized community attitudes toward teacher pay in the nineteenth century. Taxpayers are still looking for objective, tangible evidence that teachers are worth the money they are paid.

Teachers in the twenty-first century continue to labor, it seems, in the shadow of centuries-old attitudes toward pay and compensation. In a mobile society, they are tied to compensation practices that preclude mobility. In a workforce that is almost equally split between genders, teachers are still often paid as if theirs is a "second" salary, intended to supplement the "real" wage of a spouse. And in a profession where success is often qualitative and subjective, communities still seek to reward teachers based on bottom-line scores on standardized tests.

TEACHER COMPENSATION TODAY

In the past several decades there have been widespread efforts to rethink the structure of teacher pay. Reformers have put forward a number of proposals for changing the traditional single-salary schedule by eliminating it or supplementing the criteria for assessing pay.[11] These proposals have clustered around three types of alternative compensation systems: pay for performance, knowledge- and skills-based pay, and compensation for certification by the National Board for Professional Teaching Standards. Aspects of each of these plans have been embraced by constituencies as various as the American Federation of Teachers, the Republican party, and the Consortium for Policy Research in Education, a group of universities that includes Harvard, Stanford, and the Universities of Pennsylvania, Michigan, and Wisconsin. From a teacher's perspective, each of these alternative compensation measures is potentially problematic:

Pay for performance is perhaps the oldest of the current proposals. This approach links teacher pay to certain preset benchmarks, most often student outcomes on district or state standardized tests. Under such a plan, the single-salary schedule would be wholly or partly replaced by individual contracts; each contract would be correlated to the objective performance of the teacher's students. Conservatives argue that pay-for-performance creates the necessary incentives for teachers to focus their energy in areas that produce the most visible results.

A second alternative compensation system is pay based on "knowledge and skills." This system rewards teachers not for improving student test scores but for passing content-based proficiency tests that measure teachers' knowledge in their subjects or in new areas of pedagogy. This approach has become increasingly popular in recent years, as the Educational Testing Service (ETS) and other testing agencies scramble to develop new forms of objective measures for teacher proficiency. Currently, Ohio and Colorado use these kinds of assessments, called Praxis or INTASC (Interstate New Teacher Assessment and Support Consortium), to determine pay increases.

Most of these plans are merely repackaged versions of the merit pay systems of the 1980s. Merit pay failed to improve schools in the past for the same reasons that pay-for-performance and knowledge-and-skills-based pay schemes could easily fail today. In the first place, such approaches were often underfunded. In the 1980s, districts tended to change the criteria for awarding merit pay based on the size of the budget in any given year. In one district in Texas, where a merit system was instituted in the mid-1980s, teachers found that the criteria for becoming a "master teacher" in a new merit program were steadily increased in each year of the program's implementation.

Other problems inherent in merit-based systems included the use of cryptic assessment procedures for determining excellence and a perception that favoritism could not be eliminated as a factor in the choice of merit recipients.[12] Teachers in affluent districts more frequently received merit pay than did those in the more challenging schools in poor or urban areas, simply because the wealthier schools could afford to designate more teachers as outstanding. Quotas were used in determining quality. Finally, research on failed pay-for-performance systems in the 1980s found that student performance changed little if at all based on its implementation. The only consistent outcome was the depression of teacher morale—the factor that, more than any other, influences the quality of learning.[13]

Another alternative compensation approach is tied to certification through the National Board for Professional Teaching Standards (NBPTS). Many teachers who complete the national board certification process are rewarded with substantial bonuses from state funds. The NBPTS evaluation procedure is expensive, currently over $2,000, a cost generally borne by the individual. Most teachers would find the sum prohibitive. The test is also quite arduous; some teachers report spending more than 300 hours preparing for it, an investment of time that would be untenable for many teachers working with large classes and multiple preparations.[14]

Conservative groups have tended to support alternative pay initiatives based on merit or performance measures, while unions tend to hold fast to the single-salary schedule. Recently, however, unions have softened their stand on many of the proposals suggested above. Supplemental pay for knowledge and skills, for example, is supported by the American Federation of Teachers, as long as the criteria are made fully transparent. The great fear of the unions is that any movement away from the hard-won structures of traditional salary schedules will open the profession to exploitation—to payment based on the whims of administrators or school boards or on the ability of individual teachers to invest noncontracted time and personal money in the process. History shows that those fears are not unfounded.

A PROPOSED SALARY STRUCTURE FOR A TEACHER-CENTERED SCHOOL

Our recommendations for compensation are predicated on the notion that teachers in teacher-centered schools are well trained and have been hired through arduous recruitment and rigorous screening. Futhermore, they are required to justify their salaries through a rigorous process of evaluation, including a revised system of tenure and promotion. Based on these assumptions, we propose the following modest reforms:

1. Raise teacher base pay.

In order to attract a strong pool of qualified candidates, the starting salary for teachers must be increased, so it is comparable to that of a beginning accountant or banker. New recruits should be receiving approximately 20 percent more than they currently do. By substantially closing the gap between teachers' wages and those of other professionals in the community, bright graduates will not be able to dismiss the profession out of hand, based only on the inadequacy of the salary.

2. Do away with front-loaded salaries.

Salaries must move forward in consistent increments, so teachers have an incentive to stay in the field over time. A salary that triples by the end of a career acknowledges the value of veteran teachers, their expertise and importance to the community, and it also allows the community to demand continued hard work from veteran teachers. The assumption should be that the longer you teach, the better you are, the harder you work, and the more you get paid.

3. Maintain a clear and transparent salary schedule.

One of the many rewards of being a teacher is the sense of collegiality that can develop among like-minded intellectuals or individuals who share a love of children. The best schools are invariably those where teachers have developed a culture of mutual respect and support. Teachers in such schools share advice and resources; they socialize together; they see colleagues' problems or successes as opportunities to help or to celebrate. Such schools seem like small utopian communities, where, despite humble circumstances, participants share the best of themselves with one another. The worst schools are places where teachers are pitted against one another, through competition and the unequal distribution of scant resources.

Nothing promotes discord among teachers so readily as the sense that rewards are unfairly distributed. Teachers know they are underpaid, and many live with the daily challenges of earning a teacher's salary. An opaque and mysterious system of merit rewards effectively undermines collegiality; this is the main reason why unions have held so vehemently to the notion of a single pay schedule.

4. Provide supplemental pay for service.

A transparent system of compensation does not preclude additional pay for service, however. While all teachers with equivalent years of experience and education would fall at the same level on the salary scale, teachers should be able to earn additional income by being elected to faculty or administrative committees designed to develop the curriculum, work on the schedule, mentor new teachers, and do many other tasks currently assigned to expensive administrators. Teachers would serve on these committees for a discrete term—say, three years—during which time they would be paid supplemental wages for the additional work. By requiring that faculty be elected to these committees, schools could ensure that competent people end up in decision-making positions; no one knows better than other teachers who among their ranks are most competent. Term limits would ensure that no one could monopolize the authority and income associated with these committees.

The benefits of a pay-for-service approach to school governance are obvious: First, it affords extra income to teachers who need it. Second, it dramatically reduces district expenses by reallocating the work of highly paid administrators into the hands of small subgroups of faculty. The stipends paid to teachers on these committees—even if they were exceptionally generous—

would not come close to the salary and benefits of a single administrator.[15] Third, such a committee structure would have a salutary affect on the faculty as a whole by undercutting the present two-tiered system. Faculty participation in the running of a school creates a sense of community that is difficult to achieve in any other way.

5. Make tenure financially meaningful.

A transparent salary schedule would not compromise quality. As we discuss in greater detail in a later chapter, the tenure process needs to be revised in public education. The probationary term for teachers should mirror that of colleges and universities and be expanded from three to six years, making the granting of tenure a meaningful event. That transition should bring a substantial raise, perhaps 10 percent of the teacher's salary, above cost of living increases. The prospect of such an increase would offset, we contend, some of the chronic attrition that occurs in the field.[16]

6. Make pensions portable and revise Social Security laws.

Finally, it is crucial that states revisit the laws regarding the portability of pensions, allowing teachers who are not yet fully vested in a given state to transfer years of service to a second state. There is no reason why teachers, in our modern, mobile society, must sacrifice the pension monies due them because they relocate to another state to care for an aging parent or follow a transferred spouse. Similarly, teachers who are vested in one state should be allowed to bring that pension with them to another, combining their benefits across both states. In an era when good teachers are increasingly hard to find, a lack of pension portability functions as a disincentive to continue teaching for those who must move from one geographic region to another. Though statistics are not available, it stands to reason that individuals who are forced to sacrifice their pensions will be less inclined to remain in the field. The country would be well served by instituting a national pension system for teachers.

Problems with the Social Security laws also make it difficult for teachers to move from state to state. According to the Windfall Elimination Provision, teachers stand to lose a significant percentage of their Social Security benefits if they move from a state that does not participate in the system. The National Education Association is campaigning to revoke this law, which penalizes public employees in unnecessary ways. Other laws, like the government pension offset law, is similarly illogical and punitive. This law denies widows and widowers in public service professions significant percentages of their Social Security survivor benefits (they lose two-thirds of the benefits) because they work in states where public employees do not participate in the Social Security system. This law, which was instituted in 1977 as a federal cost-cutting measure, penalizes teachers at a most vulnerable time in their careers. Indeed, many teachers do not even realize the law exists until they are notified of the penalty after the death of their spouse.

These may seem like minor concerns in the overall scheme of teacher compensation, but they contribute materially and symbolically to the general sense that teachers are expendable, that their work is not valuable, and that their compensation is an afterthought of a society distracted by more pressing concerns than education.

7. Offer incentives to attract the best teachers to the most difficult schools.

Better salaries may not be sufficient to attract top candidates to every school in America. Many urban or rural poor schools, the ones that most need the best teachers, will require special incentive pay, beyond what is offered in the average suburban school. Such schools too often attract the least-qualified individuals or resort to Teach for America candidates, whose commitment to the field is often fleeting and whose poor preparation for teaching renders them vulnerable to burnout.

Teachers in high-risk schools need to come from the very best schools themselves. They need to be talented and committed, professionally certified, and, ideally, armed with graduate degrees in the teaching of their subjects. Such teachers should start work at salaries that acknowledge the skills, stress, and importance of their labor—salaries equivalent to those earned by starting lawyers, architects, and corporate executives.

In addition to cash incentives, teachers who work in these schools (both new teachers and talented veterans recruited from other districts and states) should receive subsidized housing and low-interest loans to purchase homes in the community. These loans would remain in effect as long as the teacher remained employed in the school. At present, some of America's most affluent communities are already experimenting with such incentives, using local tax revenue to support these ancillary perks.[17] The only way this can happen in poor communities is through consistent corporate support or through federal and state intervention. This is the one recommendation we make that requires significant new resources.

PAYING FOR TEACHER-CENTERED SCHOOLS

The reforms outlined above do not generally require costly new government initiatives. They do require, however, that Americans rethink the way we are spending our current education dollars. Conservatives argue that the problem with American education is not a lack of funds. "We throw money at the schools," they say, "and nothing changes. We increase education budgets and the funds just disappear." To some extent, we agree with this charge. In total, over $320 billion is directed annually to public education in this country, and at every level that money is being ill-spent and squandered. But it is not being ill-spent on textbooks and materials or squandered on building maintenance or teacher salaries. It is being wasted on nonteachers and administrative bloat, oversized bureaucracies that suck up tax revenues and have little or no impact on school improvement or student learning. Teacher-centered schools put most of their money and resources into people and initiatives that have the most direct effect on students—into talented teachers' salaries, smaller class sizes, and an improved school environment. In our current system, too much money goes everywhere else.

Educational waste begins, of course, on the federal level. The Department of Education was begun in 1979 with a mere 100 employees. Today it employs over 5,000 individuals, 89.4 percent of whom were deemed nonessential during the 1995 government shutdown, and the vast majority of whom have no direct contact with teachers or students.[18] And the growth won't be stopping soon: The new Bush education bill recently allocated a 40 percent increase in the budget for the federal Department of Education.

While there is no question that a country as large and diverse as ours needs a central bureau of education and that the Department of Education serves a number of vital functions in administering important federal programs, such an elaborate and bloated bureaucracy often seems, from a teacher's perspective, to cause more harm than good. New offices with new titles and functions emerge regularly and then justify their existence by creating pointless initiatives and mandates that burden everyone they affect. New mandates require the hiring of new functionaries to disseminate them and oversee their implementation. Bloat begets bloat: Funds get spent on paperwork, secretaries, and grants that lead nowhere. And the cost is in both dollars and manpower. Teachers are forced to spend their time responding to federal bureaucratic demands instead of working with children. Building secretaries and principals waste time filling out forms that end up filed in vaults that nobody will ever open.

As an example, in 2001 the Department of Education developed new Title II regulations requiring elaborate documentation from every teacher education program in the U.S.—mandating the annual submission of names, test scores, and other information on every student enrolled in their programs. No explanation was given for why this new information was important, and no federal support was offered to institutions for collecting these data. Schools that did not comply were threatened with fines of $25,000 a year. At our own college, professors wasted hours of work compiling these statistics, which were then turned into a glossy-covered report that was sent to congressional offices, perused there by a summer intern, and tossed in the garbage. This kind of useless mandate is an insult to every struggling teacher in the country.

Distressing as it is, however, federal bloat pales in comparison to wasteful practices on the state and local levels. Here, the statistics are nothing short of astonishing. From 1960 to 1984 there was a 500 percent increase in curriculum specialists and instructional supervisors. The number of teacher aides has grown from 700,000 in 1960 to more than 2.5 million today.[19] During the same period, the overall proportion of teachers, among all professional school staff, fell from 70 percent to 52 percent. And of that 52 percent, only 43 percent were classroom teachers; the rest were special needs counselors, guidance staff, aides, and other personnel. In other industrialized countries, with whom we routinely compare our students' achievements, the percentages are quite different—60 to 80 percent of school personnel work directly with children in classrooms.[20]

According to national census polls, the average school district hires one administrator for every fifty-five teachers, and in some states the ratio is far worse. Illinois and Mississippi have teacher-to-administrator ratios of 33.4 to one. North Dakota, unbelievably, requires one administrator for every 17.7 teachers, a ratio that is far higher than most teacher-to-student ratios in American classrooms. These numbers do not include secretaries, instructional specialists, and other nonteaching support staff. Other statistics are equally disheartening: In St. Paul, Minnesota, out of every 100 school employees, only 39.5 are teachers.[21] According to a recent story in the *Detroit News,* eight Detroit school employees were promoted to executive-level positions and received pay increases between 11 and 48 percent, while at the same time Detroit teaching and support staff positions were substantially cut. Detroit public schools now have thirty-four individuals in executive director positions, earning from $98,000 to

$132,000, whose job it is to oversee the work of principals and other administrative departments, like adult education.[22] The average expenditure devoted to actual classroom teachers has decreased from 51 percent in 1960–61 to 39.2 percent in 1999–2000. The rest goes to administrator salaries, food services, transportation, central office costs, and an endless array of other departments that sustain the school bureaucracy.[23]

Many have decried such waste by asserting that funds for education should be cut. But the problem is not with bloated budgets; it is with how those budgets get allocated. Schools need to spend much more on critical factors that influence student learning and achievement. That means cutting expensive administrative positions, cutting unnecessary programming, and cutting high-stakes testing and the bureaucracy that supports it. What parent would not prefer to take her own child to school with a sandwich (eliminating the cost of both a bus and a cafeteria), if she was guaranteed a talented teacher and small class size? What parent would not prefer to have two fewer assistant superintendents of instruction in the system, if the school could then afford four additional teachers?

Constructing teacher-centered schools will require different budgetary priorities in different schools. But in every school in America, money can be redistributed to teacher salaries by enforcing a single key rule: Every educational professional in the system, every principal and vice principal, every department chair and curriculum coordinator, must be a certified teacher and must continue to teach. The two-tiered system that currently exists in the public schools is outmoded and inefficient. According to this system, poorly paid high school teachers work with up to 150 students a day, teaching five classes, while administrators earn sometimes double or triple the teacher's wage while working in offices far removed from the realities of the classroom. If the work of teaching were redistributed to all the professionals in the building, fewer teachers would be necessary, and salaries could be increased.

Other benefits accrue from requiring that administrators teach. Teachers have long noted that when those among them choose to become full-time administrators they quickly lose their capacity to empathize with their former colleagues. It is astonishing how quickly one forgets the complex stresses and challenges of teaching once one is charged with implementing bureaucratic mandates or fielding parent complaints. Even one class a day, one semester a year, is enough to retain the flavor of the work and maintain credibility with teachers—who often measure administrative effectiveness against what the principal seems to know about real teaching.

Raise salaries 20 percent. Make pensions portable. Compensate teachers for meaningful service. Require everybody to teach. These simple, logical ways to improve teacher compensation would bankrupt no district in America, and they would have a real, measurable impact on teacher quality and morale.

NOTES

1. Edward Liu, Susan M. Kardos, David Kauffman, Heather G. Peske, and Susan Moore Johnson, "Barely Breaking Even: Incentives, Rewards, and the High Costs of Choosing to Teach" (Harvard University School of Education, Cambridge, Mass., July 2000), http://www.gse.harvard.edu/~ngt/Barely%20Breaking%20Even%200700.PDF. The research for this paper was conducted by the Project on the Next Generation of Teaching and funded by the Spencer Foundation. Using a qualitative method, the researchers interviewed a diverse group of first- and second-year teachers in Massachusetts public schools, paying close attention to differences between first career and midcareer. The researchers found that while money "is not the primary incentive to enter teaching—intrinsic rewards provide the main incentive—it can serve as a disincentive or a barrier for those who might otherwise be attracted to teaching." Moreover, the teachers they interviewed asserted that "the costs of entering (and remaining in) teaching are quite high and very discouraging" (p. 3). Although the respondents chose teaching in spite of the low pay, many worry about being able to "afford" to teach and are "uncertain if they will stay in the profession longer" (p. 17). Although they "very much wanted to stay in teaching, they wondered whether, by accepting so much less money than other professions they were doing themselves and their families a disservice"

(p. 17). The study concluded that to recruit the 2.2 million teachers needed in the next decade, salaries would have to be increased. The study also asserted that given the low rewards of teaching many prospective teachers did not want to pay for teacher training programs (p. 17). And who can blame them! Would doctors pay the high costs of medical school if the rewards of their profession were so paltry?

2. Richard M. Ingersoll, "Teacher Turnover and Teacher Shortages: An Organizational Analysis," *American Educational Research Journal* 38, no. 3 (fall 2001): 499–534. Ingersoll found that the compensation structure is one of the key reasons teachers give up the profession.

3. Brian Crosby, *The 100,00-Dollar Teacher: A Teacher's Solution to America's Declining Public School System* (Sterling, Va.: Capital Books, 2002), 105–36.

4. Albert Shanker, "The End of the Traditional Model of Schooling and a Proposal for Using Incentives to Restructure Our Public Schools," *Phi Delta Kappan* 71, no. 5 (January 1990): 345–57.

5. Liu et al., "Barely Breaking Even." The study asserts that "for highly educated individuals, choosing to teach has always meant forgoing higher paying alternatives. However, now more than ever, this career decision requires significant sacrifices" (p. 2).

6. American Federation of Teachers, AFL-CIO, *Survey and Analysis of Teacher Salary Trends 2000*, http://www.aft.org/research. See also Dan D. Goldhaber, "How Has Teacher Compensation Changed?" in *Selected Papers in School Finance* (Washington, D.C.: Urban Institute, 2000–01), http://nces.ed.gov/pubs2001/2001378_2.pdf. Goldhaber found that "over the long term, relative teacher compensation plays an important role in influencing the decision to enter and leave the profession" (p. 5). Expressed interest in teaching as a career tends to track closely with fluctuations in relative teacher salaries.

7. The first formal schools appeared in the 1630s. The Boston Latin School, established in 1635, is usually considered the first town-supported school with a continuous history. It established a pattern of local control that was further strengthened by passage in Massachusetts of the Old Deluder Satan Act of 1647, which required every town of at least 50 households to hire a teacher of reading and writing and those of 100 or more households to establish and operate a grammar school as well. Intended to advance literacy so that all could possess "knowledge of the Scriptures," the act expressed the colonists' desire to preserve learning amid the wilderness conditions of their communities.

8. Rosetta Cohen and Samuel Scheer, eds., *The Work of Teachers in America: A Social History through Stories* (Mahwah, N. J.: Lawrence Erlbaum, 1997), 13–35. The book includes first-hand accounts of colonial schools by John Trumbull (1750–1831), Phillip Freneau (1752–1832), and Royall Tyler (1757–1826). All of the writers comment on the poor salaries of teachers, who were sometimes paid in rye or corn instead of hard currency.

9. Willard Waller, *The Sociology of Teaching* (New York: Wiley, 1932), 54.

10. Some states' pension plans, like the one in Connecticut, give credit to teachers for years of service in other states, provided that they pay for those years immediately prior to their retirement. The costs are prohibitive because the retiring teacher must essentially pay both the principal and the interest that the money would have earned in the pension fund from the time the teacher began teaching in the state. It would be a great enticement for experienced teachers to continue their careers in a new state if they could "purchase" their years of prior service as soon as they begin teaching. If that were the case, teachers could roll over their pension funds and have hopes of being able to earn a decent pension upon retirement. New Jersey currently makes such provisions.

11. Brad Goorian, "Alternative Teacher Compensation." November 2000, Eric Digest 142, ERIC, ED 446368, http://eric.uoregon.edu/publications/digests/digest142.html.

12. Jerry Jesness, "Teacher Merit Pay," *Education Week* (4 April 2001), http://www.edweek.org/ew/ewstory.cfm?slug=29jesness.h20. Commenting on the merit pay system begun in Texas in 1984 and abandoned in 1992, Jessness writes: "If a teacher drew a rough class and an unsympathetic principal, she could kiss her bonus goodbye. The same could go for teachers who graded too harshly or refused to incorporate the latest pedagogical fads into their teaching. For example, those who resisted the whole-language-reading tide, then considered to be the bright future of literacy, could be punished by having their career-ladder stipends revoked. Ditto for those who refused to pad grades, give preferential treatment to star athletes, narrowly teach to standardized tests, or compromise their academic integrity by catering to the whims of administrators and parents."

13. Linda Lumsden, "Teacher Morale," March 1998, Eric Digest 120, ERIC, ED 422601. Lumsden cites studies that conclude that

"where morale was high, schools showed an increase in student achievement." Conversely, she asserts, "low levels of satisfaction and morale can lead to decreased teacher productivity and burnout " (p. 1).

14. Diane Barone, ed., *The National Board Certification Handbook: Support and Stories from Teachers and Candidates* (York, Me.: Stenhouse Publishing, 2002), 13.

15. Charles Osgood, "Teachers in Residence" (ACF Newsource, July 2001), http://www.acfnewsource.org/education/teachers_resi dence. Osgood reports that in California the Silicon Valley Manufacturing Group has been working with nearby cities to aid teachers in purchasing first homes. Osgood writes: "In San Ramon, California, where a development company created the 'tutors in housing projects' concept. A. F. Evans Company is offering ten half-price apartments to teachers in the newly refurbished Monterey Pines complex in Richmond, California, in exchange for those teachers tutoring their neighbors for two hours a week. The idea is to do something to help teachers as well as bring a sense of stability and community to the complex, which just a few years ago had a reputation for being a den for drug dealing and crime. The former JFK Manor was described by the H.U.D. as the worst subsidized housing project in Northern California. The A. F. Evans Company bought the property relatively cheaply, evicted some tenants, ended the federal subsidy program, refurbished the 324-unit building, and renamed it. The company approached the West Contra Costa County school district with the idea, but officials were initially skeptical because they had heard about the shootings and drug dealings at the old JFK Manor. However, after the school officials saw how the developer transformed the complex, they were quickly persuaded to use the half-off rent offer as a selling point in the school district's teacher recruiting efforts. Dave Luongo, an English teacher from Boston who is now teaching at Kennedy High in Richmond, is the first teacher to become a "teacher in residence." He pays just $450 a month for a spacious two-bedroom apartment that's brand new inside. . . . Luongo hears stories about the drug dealing and shootings that happened there but says the place is nothing like that now."

16. Ingersoll, "Teacher Turnover." See also a discussion of Ingersoll's work in *Teacher Quality Policy Briefs* 3 (January 2001), http://depts.washington.edu/ctpmail/PDFs.Breifthree.pdf. The study reports: "After three years 29 percent of all beginning teachers have left teaching altogether, and after five years, 39 percent."

17. National Center for Home Education, Issue Alert (12 January 2000), http://nche.hslda.org. In the decade prior to the establishment of the Department of Education, spending on education rose at only about half the rate of the rest of the nondefense discretionary budget (35 percent vs. 65.4 percent). In the period since the establishment of the department, education spending has risen at a rate over three times as fast as that of nondefense discretionary programs (29.5 percent vs. 7.9 percent).

18. U.S. Department of Education, *Digest of Educational Statistics* (Washington, D.C., 2000). The Department reports that the average assistant superintendent earns $88,913. If a district hired one fewer such administrator and delegated his work to a small group of strong teachers, it would save money and energize the faculty by providing them with greater professional status.

19. Martin L. Gross, *Conspiracy of Ignorance: The Failure of American Schools* (New York: HarperCollins, 1999), 30.

20. Linda Darling-Hammond, "Teacher Quality and Student Achievement: A Review of State Policy Evidence," *Education Policy Analysis Archives* 8 (January 2000), http://epaa.asu.edu/epaa/v8n1/.

21. Mark Antonucci, "Tribute for a Light: Public Education Spending and Staffing" (Education Intelligence Agency, May 2001): 16–17. http//members.aol.com/educintel/eia/Tribute/table9.pdf.

22. Michigan Education Report (30 May 2000), http://www.educationreport.org/pubs/mer/article.asp?ID=4366.

23. Crosby, *The 100,000-Dollar Teacher*, 225.

CHAPTER 3

Environment

The work environment, those attitudes and mores, both tangible and ineffable, that pervade the classroom and the school as a whole, are critical factors influencing teacher morale, longevity, and commitment. We know that teachers happily stay in the profession when the work environment is positive, even when salaries are not competitive. We also know that they move from school to school more often because of environmental issues than economic ones.[1]

Given the evidence, then, one would assume that policy makers would frequently search for ways to improve the working conditions for teachers in schools, that grateful taxpayers, relieved to know that money is not necessarily the key concern of teachers, would seek other strategies to support them. This, of course, is not the case. When taxpayers, policy makers, parents, and administrators do talk about improving the school environment, they talk only about children. "Kids need bigger lockers." "Kids need to feel safe and comfortable." Children may well need these things, but teachers need them too—as much, if not more. Teachers are older, wearier, less resilient, more sensitive to disorder and ugliness. Children spend four to six years in most school buildings. Teachers spend twenty-five to thirty. What is more, teachers' moods and morale dominate classroom life. Their view of the work environment directly impacts the quality of student instruction and, by extension, the level of student achievement. A teacher-centered school, then, is a school where students are most likely to succeed because the environment is calculated to please—first and foremost—the adults in the building.

THE WORK LOAD

The most basic way in which the school environment can be improved is to rethink the teacher's work load. The average class size in America varies dramatically from school to school and community to community. Affluent public schools boast average class sizes of fifteen or seventeen, with advanced or AP classes having as few as six or seven. We all know, though, that the country is filled with classrooms on the other extreme: Classes with thirty-five or forty-five students in them; classes held in auditoriums without amplification, in boiler rooms without ventilation, and in bathrooms. It is not uncommon for a teacher in an urban high school to have 150 students and five classes a day. But even in middle-class suburban schools, the work load is only slightly easier. Most high school teachers work with 120 to 140 students a day. We challenge anyone—no matter how brilliant or how well paid—to work effectively with so many adolescents at one time. Such demands wear teachers down and compromise their effectiveness.

In a teacher-centered school, elementary school teachers would be assigned no more than twenty students in a class. High school teachers would work with no more than eighty students a day, with four academic class periods instead of five, and no more than three separate preparations in any given semester. As any teacher will tell you, even this work load is a challenge; it is simply a reasonable challenge.

A second drain on teacher productivity is the system of imposed "duties" that are built into the contract of most elementary and secondary teachers. In addition to teaching, most public school faculty are also required to monitor, during their one free period, rowdy study halls and stairwells, outdoor lounge areas, bathrooms, and an assortment of other unpleasant sites. Administrators often claim that such ancillary responsibilities allow teachers to get to know kids outside the classroom. This may be true. But too often the policing nature of the duty simply forces kids to resent adults, to see them only as punitive and voyeuristic.

Teachers should indeed interact with students outside the classroom, and requiring them to spend time with kids in cafeterias and study halls is not unreasonable. But such duties need to be redefined to protect the integrity and dignity of the teachers' role. In a teacher-centered school, all faculty and staff would be required to "dine" with students once a week. That would mean sitting with them and engaging students in conversation over a civil lunch. All faculty and staff might also be asked to offer study hall support once a week. This would mean providing homework help, answering questions, and modeling for students the ways in which mature people read and work in such a setting.

Students who are chronically disruptive and incapable of using their time productively should not be allowed to remain in study halls. It most certainly should not be the responsibility of a teacher to continuously silence and harangue such students. University and college professors often perform service to their institutions by dining occasionally in the student dormitories. They are often asked to monitor math or writing centers to offer support. Schoolteachers should be required to do this work—more formally and consistently, perhaps—but in the same spirit: as mentors, expert helpers, and adult friends, not as security guards, prison wardens, or angry parents.

A CIVIL WORKPLACE

American teachers, more often than not, spend their days in what any other professional might consider a "hostile" workplace. Indeed, the lack of physical privacy in many schools, the exceptionally spartan conditions of lavatories and dining spaces, the quality of equipment and resources would certainly incense an entry-level lawyer, beginning architect, or corporate executive. What is more, were the acceptable norms for behavior and language, the rules regarding cursing, shouting, and abusive speech replicated in a corporation or business, it might present grounds for lawsuits. There is rightly much concern for the well-being of children in the physical spaces of schools. We worry about the presence of drug dealers on school grounds and speak with passionate concern about the rise of student violence. What is less frequently discussed is that these same factors influence the work of teachers, as do a myriad of other less grave dangers like ego assaults and insubordination.

In order to make meaningful changes in the environment of the school, two entrenched norms of school life will need to be dramatically altered: the civil environment of the school—the culture of disrespect, lethargy, and violence; and the physical environment of the school—the work space where teachers spend their careers.

THE PROBLEM OF DISCIPLINE

Children misbehave, and teenagers break rules. This is a fact of life, and no one expects individuals who have devoted their lives to working with children to abdicate all responsibility for dealing with those realities. Teachers need to keep order in their classrooms and to understand the psychology of youth well enough to bring unruly students back in line or to refocus distracted behavior. At no point in the history of the profession, however, has the teacher's role been defined as that of policeman, warden, or prison guard. Yet in many schools this is precisely the nature of their work. In some schools, the policing role is played out in subtle ways: The teacher asks for silence, and some students never comply. The teacher asks that students begin a task, and some habitually fail to respond, put their heads on their desks or turn away. In many other schools, teachers must contend with a continuous environment of disruptiveness, continuous noise while they are speaking, or habitual tardiness. Students saunter into class late, without even the pretense of an excuse. Teachers are threatened, mocked, and ignored. Everyone associated with schools knows this is true, but rarely does anyone speak openly about it. It is simply accepted as part of the culture of the profession. Such behavior, day after day, is psychologically wearing on even the most robust and optimistic teacher.

An outsider looking in on such a culture might rightly ask:

Where are the laws that govern conduct in the school? Why are students allowed to behave like this without some consequences? In any other public environment, such behavior would be deemed antisocial at best, perhaps even illegal. If a young person entered a bank, for example, loudly cursing or singing at the top of his lungs, he would be quickly escorted out of the building by a security guard. If he resisted requests to leave, he would be arrested for disturbing the peace. Why is such behavior routinely tolerated in public schools?

A HISTORY OF TEACHER AUTHORITY

One explanation for the weak civil standards that pervade American schools can be found in the social norms of the late 1960s and early 1970s. Scholars of American education see these decades as marking a pivotal shift in the relations among students, teachers, and parents. As scholars have pointed out, the rise of the various rights movements, in the wake of the Civil Rights era, ultimately undermined the traditional power of teachers.[2] While teachers may never have had the privileges associated with high social rank or wealth, they were granted, until the late 1960s, a kind of romantic status, a sentimental power derived from the popular perception of their role as nurturers. The sociologist Dan Lortie calls the place of the teacher in mid-twentieth century society "special, but shadowed"[3]; Teachers were respected as experts in the domain of children, even as they were shadowed by their low wages and limited sphere of influence.

Other scholars, like Gerald Grant, refer to the former influence of teachers as deriving from what he calls "traditional, legal/rational, and charismatic" authority, forms of authority granted to teachers by the communities they served.[4] Grant equates the teacher's "traditional authority" with that of a parent: Historically, teachers acted *in loco parentis*, and their decisions with regard to children were as rarely questioned as a parent's would be. "Legal/rational authority" is defined by Grant as the power of a policeman—the power of one charged with maintenance of accepted laws. In the past, if a teacher told a student to leave the room, he had behind his demand the full legal powers of an elaborated system of laws and regulations. Students would no sooner refuse to comply than would a driver refuse to pull over when summoned by a police officer to do so. The social consequences of misbehavior were stigmatizing. Finally, Grant defines "charismatic authority" as the power derived from personality, such as that exerted by gurus and gang leaders. Some lucky teachers are born with it and can control their classes simply by virtue of their wit or *gravitas*. Most people, however, lack the necessary élan to rule by charisma alone. For them, law and tradition have carried the weight of authority.

Beginning in the late 1960s, teachers experienced a radical stripping away of their power over children. Inspired by the student rights movement and a series of Supreme Court cases that gave young people enormous new control over the adults in their lives, teachers lost whatever symbolic power they had held over young people. In the *Gault* decision of 1967, for example, the court rejected the doctrine of *parens patriae* as the founding principle of juvenile justice. "Juvenile court history," said the decision, "has demonstrated that . . . unbridled discretion, however benevolently motivated, is frequently a poor substitute for principle and procedure."[5] As a consequence of the ruling, students were afforded the same due process rights as adults in all controversies involving school personnel. In the *Winship* decision that followed three years later, the court added a "beyond a reasonable doubt" clause to their earlier ruling, shifting the burden of proof, in any dispute, to the accuser—the teacher.[6]

After the *Winship* case, schools and teachers came to view all disciplinary decisions in a new light—as the source of potential litigation. In any disagreement between faculty and students, in which there was no third party witness, teachers now held no clear advantage. In fact, one could argue that they were now at a marked disadvantage: Age and conventional power rendered one suspect. As many well-publicized court cases made clear, the teacher's discretion within the classroom, where only other children were witness, was especially vulnerable: Students began suing teachers for unwelcome grades, for "psychic pain," and for a vast array of other grievances.

Responding to the spirit of change, in 1973 the ACLU published a handbook that outlined for parents and children their legal rights vis-à-vis the teacher and the school. Bring a third party witness when conferencing with your child's teacher, the book advised. Know your rights, and get a lawyer. "If there are not enough lawyers in your area to represent all the students who need help, you might try to get your parents and other adults to organize a service of nonlawyers trained in the law of student rights to help students in hearings and in other school matters. . . . Above all," the handbook goes on to admonish, "don't let the fact that you might not have a good court case keep you from insisting on fair treatment at all times."[7]

The handbook, a truly illuminating sociological document, assumes, in short, that the teacher is a potential enemy, a cunning adversary to be reckoned with only warily. Teachers who remember this period speak of a Copernican change in school tone: a fearful and defensive atmosphere in the teachers' room, a new concern about how and indeed whether to confront student misbehavior.[8]

Some of the reforms wrought by the student rights movement were ultimately good ones. The new laws and changed attitudes did protect children against arbitrary punishment by cruel or vindictive teachers. But it is hard not to feel that something was permanently lost in the process—something subtle and ineffable. Today, a litigious culture clearly impacts curriculum and instruction. A third of all high school principals in the last two years have been involved in student-related lawsuits, and teacher liability coverage against lawsuits has increased dramatically in the last decade.[9] Teachers are less free to be themselves, to be playful and idiosyncratic; they are also less free to maintain high standards, to teach with the integrity that makes hard work meaningful. As with all cultural change, those teachers who remained after the seventies rulings gradually became accustomed to the new norms, and few practicing teachers today remember a time when it was different. But the shift in authority still takes a toll on teachers. Even anecdotally, among our teacher friends, stories abound: No high school teacher we know will spend time alone in a classroom with only one student present; few will touch a student, not even to give him a congratulatory pat on the back. Clearly, not only does the fear of legal reprisal create an ongoing stress in the lives of teachers; it also profoundly compromises the quality of the relationships between students and teachers.

At approximately the same time that the student rights movement was challenging the discretionary power of teachers, a second rights movement was spearheading legislation that would also change the work of teachers. Public Law 94-142, the Disabilities Act, passed in 1975, brought with it a series of mandates whose impact is seen in virtually every classroom in America today. The Disabilities Act "mainstreamed" students with special needs—both physical and emotional—into regular classes. The idea of a "least restricted environment," placing the disabled child in the most normal setting possible, meant that regular classroom teachers were now asked to meet the needs of students with a great range of problems, students requiring special attention. Stipulated within that act was the creation, for these children, of "independent educational plans" (or IEPs), written by special-needs teachers and enacted by regular classroom teachers with the support of this specialized personnel.

Though Public Law 94-142 added a new and often difficult dimension to the teacher's job, few teachers would argue with the spirit of the law or the efficacy of its original design. It was not obvious at the start that such a logical and humane edict could potentially exploit teachers. As originally planned, for example, 40 percent of the costs associated with mainstreaming students with disabilities was to fall on the federal government, with 60 percent carried by state and local taxes. Today the federal government pays only 12 percent of districts' costs for special needs, even as the numbers of students diagnosed with disabilities has increased dramatically—a 30 percent increase in ten years.[10]

As originally planned, newly hired special needs personnel would work closely with teachers, advising and supporting them and bearing the burden of most of the paperwork legally required as documentation. Today, cutbacks on special needs personnel have left many teachers contending alone with growing numbers of students whose problems are increasingly complex and confounding. Bureaucratic paperwork and meetings with psychologists, counselors, and other specialists have consumed more and more of the regular classroom teacher's time, with neither the community nor the local school board acknowledging the added work associated with these responsibilities. In any other profession, if a work load is drastically increased in one area, it is necessarily reduced in another. If not, workers are compensated for the overload. This has never happened in the teaching profession.

Finally, the definition of "special needs" itself has grown and changed over time. Today the idea of "disability" embraces a vast array of antisocial behavior. Violent students, students with severe emotional problems, and even juvenile criminals are easily classified in school systems as "special needs" and are placed without assistance in mainstream classes. Getting those students removed from classrooms takes enormous time and places schools at tremendous risk for liability.[11]

Violence and the threat of it are not confined, of course, to urban inner-city schools. The Columbines aside, an extraordinary number of teachers in America have been physically threatened in some way or had their property vandalized at some point in their careers. One in six teachers reports having been the victim of violence in or around the school.[12] An informal survey of our own colleagues in suburban schools yields many stories: Teachers' lives are threatened; their tires are slashed; they are purposefully shoved or tripped in crowded halls. When the student offenders are identified or caught, they remain buffered from adult penalties. Sometimes they appear back in the same classrooms they have disrupted, still assigned to the same teachers they have threatened or even assaulted. Teachers have no say in this matter. They are passive recipients of decisions made by the central office, or the school's psychological counseling staff, or the courts. Is it any wonder that the National Educational Association has recently added a "homicide benefit" to its insurance package for teachers, in response to growing fears about being murdered on the job?[13]

PROPOSED CHANGES IN THE CIVIL ENVIRONMENT

For the sake of the teachers, we believe that the following changes must be made to improve the civil environment of schools. To begin, the courts need to revisit the 1975 Disabilities Act, with all its subsequent titles, and close those loopholes that allow criminals access to schools as alternatives to prison. The courts and legislature also need to reconsider the idea of "least restrictive environment" for young people whose disabilities too profoundly compromise the quality of the classroom environment for other children and for teachers. Students who cannot control themselves, whose behavior has been deemed antisocial or sociopathic by outside agencies, must not be allowed in public school classrooms.

Instead, alternative schools need to be created—like halfway houses for public education. Young people in such places should have the right to "earn" their way back into regular schools, but not until they have proved themselves capable of working with others, of respecting authority, and of following basic rules. Most decisions about reentry—when and under what conditions a formerly disruptive student can return to the regular classroom— should be made in consultation with teachers, who currently have little or no input into such matters. To facilitate this, teams of teachers might be selected to serve terms on school-based panels charged with interviewing returning students and assessing their cases, with such teachers being given compensation or a course release during the duration of their terms.

As for the more conventional disciplinary problems faced by teachers on a daily basis, these also need to be addressed in new ways. According to a well-publicized survey of public school students, 40 percent claim that their learning is compromised by chronically disruptive students—ordinary kids who undermine the environment of the classroom.[14] When students are disruptive, they should not be allowed to remain in the classroom, and punishment for their behavior should fall outside the purview of the regular classroom teacher. This change would benefit everyone involved. In many high schools (and probably the majority of them, though such statistics are impossible to gather) the unspoken disciplinary policy of the administration is that teachers should "skin their own skunks"—that is, keep their behavior problems to themselves and not burden the main office with minor offenders. In fact, untenured teachers know that principals will often evaluate their success in the classroom based largely on their disciplinary abilities. Albert Einstein would have had his contract terminated, so goes the standard teacher-joke, if he could not make the boys in the back of the room get off the radiator.

A teacher-centered school is a place where teachers teach and students learn, not where educated professionals spend their time haranguing recalcitrant children. In such schools, teachers would be perceived as "above" the mundane labor of punishment; disciplining kids would be seen for what it is: a waste of teachers' time and a misuse of their expertise.

For such a change in attitude to take place, administrators must assume new responsibility for student behavior. Principals need to communicate "outrage" when students are sent to them for disrupting a class. The school culture, communicated from the top down, must be one that assumes the teacher to be a person worthy of respect; showing disrespect for a teacher must be perceived by administrators as unacceptable and even antisocial behavior which calls for strict consequences. If administrators believed this about their faculty, if they acted upon it sincerely and consistently, students would quickly come to believe it as well.

The first step, then, in creating a teacher-centered institution includes setting a series of core policies regarding student discipline and the civil environment. We propose the following:

1. Local school boards must be allowed the discretion to deny admission to any student who has been suspended for more

than thirty days, has been expelled from another public
school, or has been dismissed for disciplinary reasons from
a private school. Alternative schools for delinquent children
should be available to take in such students, if reason dic-
tates they cannot perform in the regular school environment.

2. Any student over the age of thirteen who is habitually and
   chronically disruptive, despite interventions from teachers
   and parents, may be expelled from the school for the
   remainder of the year.

3. Students who disturb the work of others with aggressive
   and disruptive speech should be subject to fines. A child
   who walks in the hall cursing loudly should be fined seventy-five dollars for disrupting the peace.

4. Finally, fighting should be viewed as criminal assault. If a
   child is led from the school in handcuffs, others will be dis-
   suaded from fighting.

The recommendations made here do not constitute a "zero tolerance" policy. Most offending students may well be spared the
most draconian punishments. The point is that schools and teachers should have the option to impose those punishments when
and if they feel they are necessary. Schools would no longer be
held captive by child rights laws that allow psychotic and antisocial individual students to terrorize, undermine, and demoralize
teachers and students alike.

THE PHYSICAL ENVIRONMENT

The physical environment of the school, the structure and condition of the daily workplace, is an equally potent source of demoralization for teachers. Years ago, the *New York Times Magazine*
published a photographic essay comparing the conditions in prisons with the conditions of inner-city schools. The reader will
guess what the photographs demonstrated: Prisons were new and

pristine, with airy dining rooms and sports centers with swimming pools. The schools were a disgrace, dank and crumbling. Exposed pipes in the bathrooms dripped over ancient lighting fixtures, cracked sinks, and broken toilets. Windowless classrooms were unswept; ceiling tiles were missing; clocks were dangling from their wires on the wall. The essay asked us to consider what such a contrast suggested about our national priorities—and more specifically about our view of children. How could we Americans subject children to such conditions? And in doing so, how could we not expect those children to end up in the very prisons we are paying so much money to refurbish?

The images struck a deep chord with many people, though we would wager that few readers (apart from teachers) also considered what it would be like to work in such environments. The impact of such ugliness on anyone's self-esteem must be devastating. Subjected to those conditions over the course of a career, a teacher would certainly become angry, cynical, and hopeless. Jonathan Kozol, in his first great book on urban education, *Death at an Early Age,* writes about the kind of curious personality changes that began to afflict him after only several months teaching in such an environment. He began to become a kind of apologist for the school, to harangue his students about their lack of "appreciation" for all they had been granted. Teaching amidst squalor, in a classroom where the winter wind whipped through broken windows that had been hastily covered over with cardboard, Kozol found himself losing touch with his own humanity. If the children were being denied the right to decent learning conditions, the teacher was being denied access to his own feelings. He was being forced to blot out the realities of his daily environment in order to survive—to live, as it were, in a state of semi-consciousness.[15]

These are drastic conditions that exist, one hopes, in only a small percentage of American schools. But even in the "average" school, in middle-class and working-class communities all over this country, conditions of teaching are often poor. It is almost a cliché of our culture that Americans resist paying for school improvement. Indeed, one could argue that the great tradition of resistance goes back to the earliest days of the republic, when Thomas Jefferson first attempted to pass his Bill for the More General Diffusion of Knowledge. The bill, which would have required a public tax to support the maintenance of elementary schools, was defeated in the Virginia legislature three times. At first, in 1789, Jefferson excused its defeat, assuming that citizens were still skittish about the notion of taxation—even for a worthy cause. When it was defeated a third time, in 1817, he was thoroughly disgusted. He had come to see that it was not politics but parsimony that kept Americans from paying for schools.

And this has been true ever since. A recent NEA study documented over $300 billion in unmet repairs to school infrastructure.[16] When money is spent on schools, often after bitter budget fights or controversial referendums, it is most likely spent on refurbishing gymnasiums and football stadiums, buying more computers, or getting Web access into classrooms. These are all good and important expenditures. But they are expenditures that serve only the clients in the school; they do little or nothing for the teachers. For teachers in most American schools, the physical workspace is simply inadequate, and that workspace is invariably the lowest priority on any school budget. When money comes available, no one thinks about redecorating the teachers' lounge or spending a few hundred dollars to buy some new telephones for faculty offices. It is simply not a priority. Walk into the non-public areas of any small corporation or law firm, and you will usually find pleasant, clean, and attractive spaces—as attractive as the public areas used by clients and patrons. In good colleges and universities, faculty dining halls are like nice restaurants. Faculty lounges are civilized places, with phones and newspapers, overstuffed chairs, and other basic amenities. Many private schools offer faculty members their own private offices, small, secure spaces that teachers can decorate to reflect their sensibilities and fill with their own books, without fear that they will be stolen.

It is a given that in public institutions such generous allocations of space are impossible. But most schools do little or nothing to meet teachers' needs in terms of the physical environment.

Classrooms are cramped; teachers share filing cabinets with colleagues; desks, phones, and clocks are old and broken. In many schools, the only lamps, artwork, or rugs that appear in teachers' lounges or shared offices are placed there by the teachers themselves, at their own expense. Even with scant resources, teachers' workplaces can be clean, comfortable, and attractive. For that to happen, however, somebody has to care about such things. Somebody has to understand that there is a relationship between the atmosphere in the teachers' cafeteria and the quality of instruction that goes on in the classroom, a relationship between the physical work space and the capacity of a profession to attract and retain talented employees.

One logical way in which the school's physical environment can be improved is by requiring students to maintain it themselves. There is so much to be gained by including young people in the work of school maintenance, that it is hard to understand why public institutions do not do this routinely. When students are responsible for cleaning their own environment, they are, obviously, more alert to that environment. They feel more connected to it and are less likely to destroy or deface it. The physical labor of cleaning is also salutary; many students actually enjoy such work and find it a helpful antidote to studying. Maintaining the building and classrooms also gives students a basic sense of usefulness that they may not find in other endeavors. Wealthy parents pay a thousand dollars a week for their children to attend riding camps where they sweep out barns and clean horse stalls. In even the most luxurious camps, every child is required to clean his bunk and make his bed. Everyone understands that such work builds character and integrity. Finally, including students in the work of maintenance saves money on janitorial staff—money that could be used to reduce class size and increase teacher salaries.

PROPOSED CHANGES IN THE PHYSICAL ENVIRONMENT

If teachers are to be perceived as professionals, they must work in a professional setting. This is not to say that all schools should be transformed into corporate environments, with potted plants and watercoolers (though such amenities would be pleasant additions to most schools). Instead, we are suggesting that the environment in which teachers work should be supportive of the kind of work demanded of them. This means, on the most basic level, that certain amenities are crucial. If teachers are to maintain contact with parents, they need privacy and a telephone. If they are to work one-on-one with students, they need a quiet office space—or better, their own classroom that is not shared with two or three other teachers of different subjects, during different periods. If they are to teach with energy and optimism, they need a nice place to relax, a stress-free lunch period, a clean bathroom. Doctors, lawyers, architects, college professors, and private school teachers have these things. Public school teachers have a right to them as well.

SMALL SCHOOLS ARE TEACHER-CENTERED SCHOOLS

The most meaningful environmental change that would impact teacher morale and efficiency is a small school structure. The impulse to return to small schools, a movement that has been afoot for more than a decade now, is potentially a teacher-centered movement. Most teachers (like other professionals) work better in an intimate environment, where their clients are limited in number and their colleagues are physically and emotionally accessible. When schools are small, teachers necessarily have more discretionary power; their voices are heard, their decisions are more likely to be heeded, and they are happier. Indeed, the whole movement away from small schools at the beginning of the twentieth century was part of a larger impulse to withdraw power from the teacher and to remove personality from the teaching process. Large, sprawling regional schools or massive urban institutions housing thousands of individuals were created along factory models, where workers could perform scripted tasks with industrial efficiency. Such schools were essentially anti-teacher in their mission and purpose. If students could have been made to learn without the help of teachers, administrators would have gladly discarded them.

Small schools, by contrast, are potentially teacher-centered institutions, where faculty can assert their wills and personalities in ways that make teaching personal and creative. Research bears this out. A study of teacher satisfaction in small schools in Chicago, for example, showed that teacher morale was dramatically higher in such settings. Many teachers told the researchers that teaching in a small school "reminded them of why they became teachers in the first place."[17] The smaller the school, the less frequently teachers were asked to perform the tasks that most enervate them—monitoring bathrooms and chasing smokers out of stairwells.[18] Research shows that children perform better when they are known and appreciated, when their strengths are celebrated. The same is true for teachers. In small schools, teachers are more likely to be known and appreciated, heeded and revered. The payoff is positive all around.

Small schools require fewer administrators, which also impacts the quality of a school's environment: Bureaucracies are, by definition, alienating. The more hierarchical and bureaucratic an institution, the less intimate and nurturing. Large, cumbersome administrations undermine the personal and the idiosyncratic—traits that define the very best institutions. In most school districts in America, the average central office is crowded with expendable personnel—associate superintendent, assistant superintendent, director of curriculum, grants coordinator, director of special education, and director of guidance. There is often a reading coordinator, a math coordinator, a science coordinator, a director of media instruction, a personnel director, and several other high-level professionals with comparable titles. More often than not, these individuals spend their days far removed from any school, tucked into air-conditioned offices across the city. Teachers rarely derive any direct benefit from their work. Within schools themselves, there are also burgeoning numbers of nonteaching staff. Besides the principal, there are numerous vice-principals (one or two for discipline, one for curriculum), guidance personnel, psychologists, and drug counselors, sometimes supported by their own secretarial staff. This two-tiered system undermines collegiality. In a small school, where administrative roles are disseminated among faculty and administrators teach in classrooms, there is better morale, better communication, and a more positive institutional ethos.

Though teachers were not the primary consideration for the small schools movement, they can now be seen as a key justification. Architects and school planners need to ask themselves, How will this space work for adults? How will the teachers benefit from this design? How can we make this workplace better for them? Teachers must be used as consultants, as knowledgeable resources in the planning of new schools and the renovating of old ones. No one knows better than the teachers in the building what works and what doesn't work. It is to everyone's advantage to listen to them.

NOTES

1. National Council on Teacher Quality, *Teacher Quality Bulletin* 3, no. 3 (17 July 2002), http://www.nctq.org/bulletin/v3n3.html. The bulletin reports: "A new study sponsored by the National Bureau of Economic Research confirms that teachers tend to try to improve their working conditions rather than their salaries when changing schools. Says Harvard University professor of education Richard J. Murnane, "Paying people extra money to do an impossible job doesn't work, and you need to make the jobs doable such that at the end of the day, people feel glad that they're there." See also Debra Viadero, "Teachers Seek Better Working Conditions," *Education Week* (9 July 2002), http://edweek.org/ew/newstory.cfm?slug = 16pay.h21.

2. Gerald Grant, *The World We Created at Hamilton High* (Cambridge: Harvard University Press, 1988); David Tyack, *The One Best System: A History of Urban Education* (Cambridge: Harvard University Press, 1974), 50–57.

3. Dan Lortie, *School Teacher: A Sociological Study* (Chicago: University of Chicago Press, 1977), 10–13.

4. Grant, *The World We Created,* 122.

5. In re *Gault,* 387 US 1, 87, S. Ct. 1428 (1967).

6. In re *Winship,* 397 US 358, 90, S. Ct. 1068 (1970).

7. Alan H. Levine, Eve Cary, and Diane Divosky, *The Rights of Students: The Basic ACLU Guide to a Student's Rights* (New York: Baron Books, 1974), 58, 65.

8. Grant, *The World We Created.*

9. Mark Carpenter, "Education Not Litigation: The Paul D. Coverdell Teacher Liability Protection Act of 2001," Citizens for a Sound Economy, Capitol Comment 293 (21 March 2001), http://www.cse.org/informed/issues_template.php/590.htm. Carpenter writes: "It is difficult to measure the exact increase in litigation against teachers because most school districts attempt to keep such records confidential and many records are sealed to protect the privacy of minors. However, at the country's third largest insurer of teachers, Forrest T. Jones Inc., the number of teachers purchasing liability insurance has increased 25 percent in the past five years. Most teachers unions offer up to $1 million in liability coverage, yet some smaller unions are beginning to offer even larger packages in an effort to attract more members. For example, the Texas State Teachers Association provides $6 million in liability insurance."

10. Joetta L. Sack, "Schools Grapple with Reality of Ambitious Law," *Education Week* (6 December 2000), http://www.edweek.org/ew/ewstory.cfm?slug=14idea.h20. Sack reports that today more than 6 million students are identified as having disabilities under the Individuals with Disabilities Education Act (IDEA). Five of the disability categories under the IDEA have grown by 20 percent or more in the past ten years, an indication of shifts in the identification of disabilities. The categories that have experienced such marked growth are: specific learning disabilities, emotional disturbance, multiple disabilities, orthopedic impairments, and other health impairments. The last category includes students with attention deficit hyperactivity disorder, a condition that can entitle students to services under the IDEA, depending on its severity.

11. Ibid. Sack found that educators often use a simple scenario: If two high school students bring illegal drugs to school, and one is classified as disabled and one is not, the "able" student will likely be expelled. But the school would have to conduct a review to determine if the disabled student's offense was related to his or her disability, and, if so, he or she could only be suspended for a maximum of ten days. If the offense was not related to the disability, the student could be sus-

pended for up to forty-five days, but the school would have to convene an IEP (Individual Education Plan) team meeting to discuss a change in placement. Sack states: "If the school authorities chose to expel the student with disabilities, they would have to figure out a way to provide him or her with educational services, such as a home tutor or alternative school."

12. Metropolitan Life, "Survey of the American Teacher, 1999: Violence in America's Public Schools-Five Years Later," 18, http://www .metlife.com/WPSAssets/18729287961018400826V1Freport9–1999 .pdf.

13. "Teacher Offered Homicide Insurance," CNN.Com Education (26 July 2001), http://fyi.cnn.com/virtual/editions/europe/2000/roof/ change.pop/frameset.exclu de.html. The article reports on the NEA's decision to offer $150,000 worth of free homicide insurance. The union was prompted by several high-profile killings of teachers in recent years.

14. Diane Ravitch, "What Do Teenagers Want," *Forbes Magazine,* 22 October 1997. Ravitch quotes Stephen Barkley and Regina Cohn, *Getting By: What American Teenagers Really Think About Their Schools* (New York: Public Agenda, 1997). Barkley and Cohn report that seven out of ten students say there are too many disruptive youngsters in their classes, and 82 percent say that these troublemakers should be removed from regular classes so that others can learn.

15. Jonathan Kozol, *Death at an Early Age: The Destruction of the Hearts and Minds of Negro Children in Their Boston Public Schools* (Boston: Houghton Mifflin, 1967).

16. "Modernizing Our Schools: What Will It Cost?" National Education Association (June 2000), http://www.nea.org/lac/modern/ modrpt.pdf. A report by the American Institute of Architects, "Good Enough for Congress? A Pictorial Representation of Why Americans Deserve Better School Buildings" (http://www.e-architect.com/gov/ schoolpics) offers an equally gloomy description of the current state of American schools.

17. Diane Dunne Weaver, "Are Small Schools Better?" *Education World* (20 July 2000), at http://www.education-world.com/a_issues/ issues108.shtml.

18. Ibid. See also Patricia A. Walsey and others, *Small Schools, Great Strides: A Study of New Small Schools in Chicago* (New York: Bank Street School of Education, 2000), http:/www.Bankstreet.edu/

html/news/SmallSchools.pdf. Relying on the largest database assembled to date on small schools, the authors suggest that even though smallness by itself is not a cure for all that ails urban schools, policy makers can make a significant impact on a variety of important education issues (i.e., test scores, grade point average, and retention) if they integrate small schools into a comprehensive reform strategy. Moreover, the study found that "schoolteachers working in freestanding small schools consistently reported working in a better professional community" and were more committed to their work (p. 38).

CHAPTER 4

Training, Recruitment, and Hiring

The training, recruitment, and hiring of America's teachers are critical factors in maintaining American defense, preserving our values, protecting our economy, and advancing our culture. High-quality teacher training and first-class recruitment are not luxuries; they are the core necessity of our democratic and pluralistic system, a system that is under assault around the world today. Indeed, the getting and retaining of great teachers is the very definition of "homeland security."

Making a connection between the quality of schools and the perpetuation of security is an ongoing exercise for American policy makers. Hyman Rickover, at the height of the Cold War, also famously equated American defense with American education. And two decades ago, *A Nation At Risk* made much the same claim, using a near hysterical rhetoric that sent schools scrambling to raise graduation standards.[1] The difference between these earlier claims and our own is that the posited solution to the crisis is, from our perspective, much more straightforward and specific: It's all about the teachers. If quality education is at the heart of national defense—and it most certainly is—then train, recruit, and hire better teachers, and find ways to keep them in the field once you have them.

There is ample evidence that teacher quality is a critical factor in student learning. While sociologists bemoan the breakdown of the American family and the enormous influence of the peer group on a child's values and academic performance, study after study shows that teacher qualifications and class size outweigh and offset such factors. The National Commission on Teaching and America's Future found that teacher qualifications accounted for 43 percent of measured variance in math test score gains nationally. When class size is added to that number, the two combined factors outweighed the influence of home and family—including poverty and parental neglect—by a measurable percentage.[2] In New York City, differences in teacher qualifications were found to account for 90 percent of the variation in reading and math scores across demographically similar schools with different levels of achievement.[3] In California, lower test scores were correlated with the percentage of math teachers on emergency permits, and higher math scores were linked both to teacher qualifications and to their years of experience.[4]

Studies by Linda Darling-Hammond show again and again that teacher quality (as measured by the quality and extent of training) is the single critical factor in student success. Students perform most poorly in fields where their teachers are least prepared. In Wisconsin and Minnesota, where standards for teachers are high, Darling-Hammond found that students perform at the top of national rankings. In Louisiana, where 31 percent of new teachers are unlicensed and another 15 percent are hired on substandard licenses, students perform poorly on standardized tests. There is also dramatic evidence that students from economically disadvantaged families are most profoundly affected by the poor training of teachers. Not only are the teachers of these children most likely to hold emergency certifications, they are also less likely to hold degrees in their field. Given the correlation between teacher quality and student achievement, this fact would seem to put disadvantaged students at an even greater risk.[5]

TEACHER EDUCATION

The popular notion that good teachers are born knowing how to teach, or that a teacher must learn to teach merely by doing it, are destructive myths that undermine that integrity of the profession. Teaching is intellectual, skilled work. When it is done well, it is as complex and challenging as any other highly skilled profession, like medicine or trial law. You can put a bright, enthusiastic college graduate in front of a jury, without a bit of training, and hope he can make a coherent case for a client. By virtue of his charisma (and memories of law dramas watched on TV) that untrained student might even win a case or two. But that is not an argument for doing away with the requirement of attending law school and passing the bar exam. The movement for alternative certification, or for doing away with credentials altogether, is a cynical ploy to save tax money and divert attention away from the real problems with public schooling. By allowing anyone to teach, policy makers can postpone, at least for the short term, the more important question of why nobody wants to teach.

Untrained teachers struggle in their classrooms. Poorly trained teachers are more often incompetent than those with good training. Anyone who has worked as a mentor for new teachers or as a teacher educator knows this. We have taught intellectually gifted young women at one of the best colleges in the United States. Yet when most of these women first enter a classroom as student teachers, their strong academic prowess serves them hardly at all. Without knowledge of pedagogy, without an understanding of how children learn, without a clue about adolescent psychology, they are at sea. It is amazing to see how quickly a young person's passion and enthusiasm—those traits so touted by advocates of alternative certification—wane when students are calling out and wandering around the classroom. A recent poignant editorial in the *New York Times* gave eloquent testimony to the experiences of such new, untrained teachers. The writer, a former investment banker who entered teaching through New York's emergency certification route, wrote sadly:

> The inexperience of many New York City teachers, including me, contributes its own problems to this complicated tangle. Many of the almost eight thousand new teachers that the Board of Education hired last September were surely no more trained for the job than I was. I believed I was prepared to head a class, but a strong academic background and years in an office are not preparation for

teaching, and the Board's apparent strategy of balancing new hires' enthusiasm against their inexperience is ineffective. The turnover rate is so high that a school's "veteran" teachers have frequently been around only three years, which makes it hard for new teachers to find experienced ones.[6]

While there is no question that teacher education is important, there is also no question that poor teacher education is of little value. While it is true that teacher training has earned its lowly reputation in part because the teaching of children is simply not respected in the country, it is also true that many teacher education programs have been genuinely awful—anti-intellectual, filled with blather and rhetoric, and lacking in rigor and cohesiveness. Such programs tend to attract weak students and produce weak teachers, who then perpetuate, in the public imagination, all the negative stereotypes about the discipline of education. If shoddy medical schools accepted indifferent students into their ranks, and then produced ineffective doctors, we would look cynically on medical education as well. But bright college graduates placed in rigorous teacher education programs can emerge as first-class teachers.

What should such programs teach? New teachers need to know how children learn. The field of cognitive science has grown dramatically over the past twenty years, and a teacher who knows nothing about the way a child's mind processes information is at a disadvantage. How students come to understand and how they make meaning from the environment is of critical importance to any teacher. Teachers also need to know about child development, the emotional and physical lives of children. A new teacher armed with real understanding about the inner lives of fifteen-year-olds will have fewer discipline problems in her classroom—guaranteed. Though teachers will always encounter students whose problems fall outside the scope of a child development class, this does not preclude the value of the science for prospective teachers. Child development offers a new teacher a vital framework on which to hang her experiences with children. It is of critical importance if a teacher is going to connect emotionally with children on more than a charismatic level.

The history of the field and the laws that currently govern it are also important pre-service knowledge. In choosing to teach, one is choosing to enter a culture that possesses its own mythology and philosophy, its own politics, and its own laws. A knowledge of educational history arms the teacher against the lure of quick fixes and flashy reforms. The history of education is filled with cautionary tales about programs and policies that came and went without a whimper. Many of those policies resurface under new names, and a teacher needs to be able to recognize them. At the same time, some of the greatest thinkers in history have written about education in ways that are profound and useful. While cognitive science moves the field forward in certain ways, our understanding of human nature remains unchanged, more than justifying the value for a student of reading Plato, Rousseau, and Dewey on the subject of education. Teachers also need to enter the field knowing about the laws that impact their work, and about the ways that politics, local budgeting, and federal and state curricular policies will impact them.

Teachers need to know about learning disabilities, and about the challenges faced by second-language learners. A colleague of ours, a teacher who found her way into her district through alternative certification, tells of how she spent a full year haranguing a low-level class about their repeated and "stupid" errors, only to find out in the spring that a number had been dyslexic—a term she came to know only through a chance conversation with another teacher. The numbers of students in public schools with diagnosed learning problems is conservatively estimated at more than 13 percent of the student population.[7] The majority of these children are mainstreamed in regular classrooms to work with teachers who receive little or no support for meeting their special needs. All teachers must come into the field armed with at least a passing understanding of the nature of learning disabilities and the strategies used to help such children. This is not information to be gleaned through brief in-service training. It is too important to be learned informally.

Similarly, teachers need to be schooled in strategies for working with second-language learners. Today, more than 2 million students enrolled in American schools are classified as having limited English proficiency.[8] With cutbacks in bilingual and even ESL programs, the numbers of students who come to class with only the barest understanding of the language will certainly be growing. A generation ago such children were simply ignored, encouraged to fend for themselves. That is no longer possible. Teachers must be taught how to juggle the needs of these students along with those of everyone else.

Finally, teachers must have good and extended field experiences before they become full-fledged professionals. Student teaching with a good mentor is absolutely crucial as a rite of passage and as a critical learning experience for a novice. There is enormous evidence to support the value of such experiences and equally voluminous evidence to show that those who have inferior, abbreviated, or even no clinical experience are at a tremendous disadvantage; they are less competent, less confident, and highly susceptible to attrition.[9] Quite apart from the research, however, plain logic suggests that this is so: We would not let a lawyer argue cases in front of juries without pretrial experience. We would not let a doctor enter an operating room without years of residencies and internships. If it is to be done well, teaching is a profession that requires comparable skill and expertise.

This is the minimum of what should be required in the way of professional preparation. To say that teachers don't need this training is absurd; to say they will learn it on the job is to dismiss the hundreds of children who must suffer with these teachers before they happen to become acquainted, through trial and error, with "right practice."

In a world where teacher-centered schools are the norm, finding talented graduates of such programs will be far less difficult than it is today. With higher salaries, better working conditions, and the cachet that goes along with teaching, more talented young people will choose to become certified. One need only look to those European and Asian countries where teachers are respected and supported to see a plausible scenario for America's schools. In such countries, teacher education, which is often far less sophisticated than it is in the United States, is neither maligned nor dismissed.

TEACHER TESTING

The bottom line is that teacher-centered schools must be staffed by professionals who are certified and well educated. This means that teachers need, as a minimum, a major in a liberal arts field and certification from a teacher education program. That certification could be acquired through undergraduate coursework or, better, through a fifth year of study or a master's degree program. We also believe that teachers need to pass state competency tests, as do lawyers and doctors. Testing at this entry point serves to formalize an understanding of what a new teacher needs to know; it helps to weed out incompetents who may have slipped through poor teacher education programs; it raises the cachet of the profession in the eyes of taxpayers; and it intrudes little on the integrity or structure of teacher education programs. Tests should measure knowledge within the subject area as well as understanding of the research, policies, and history outlined above. Students who fail such tests should be able to retake them as many times as they want, and certified teachers moving from state to state should be asked to pass state tests before assuming full-fledged teacher status in their new schools.

RECRUITING

The problem of recruiting high-quality teachers is at the heart of the present-day crisis in education. But for all the hand-wringing associated with recruitment, there is much disingenuousness as well. Even in this present "crisis state," even within the context of paltry budgets, many districts in this country do an appalling job of recruiting. When a school hires a teacher, it is often hiring a lifelong colleague who will have extraordinary power over the minds of thousands of young people. And yet the effort put forth in many schools is equivalent to the hiring of a fast-food employee.

The experience of a veteran advanced-placement history teacher we know is typical of the present state of public school recruitment. Ann was a respected and highly skilled veteran who announced to her district in March that she was retiring. Indeed, under the terms of her contract she was obliged to give notice in March, ostensibly to allow sufficient time for a comprehensive search for a replacement. Ann then proceeded to wait for the announcement of the job opening. She looked everywhere—in the local and regional papers, in the professional journals and magazines that she subscribed to. Ann lives near two large eastern cities, and she assumed that the district would place an ad in at least one of the large-circulation papers in the region. Nothing appeared anywhere in March, April, or May. Nothing appeared in June or July. In the second week of August, a small ad appeared in the local gazette, reading: "Teacher, history, full-time." "Thirty-five years of experience," Ann said, "and my job comes down to this: sandwiched between Tag Sale Coordinator and Truck Driver. A tiny notice, and posted too late for me to have any say in who gets picked." Ann was replaced within a week with a graduate of the local college, one of only two candidates to apply for the job.

In a teacher-centered school, the work of recruitment would become the highest priority of the institution. If teachers are the key to educational success, then finding the best ones must be paramount. Administrators need to be literally obsessed with this task; budgets need to be reallocated to place recruitment front and center. Teachers who know both the subject and the students to be served need to be involved in the process.

In academia, candidates learn of openings through national trade journals (where ads are not expensive) or through national conferences, which serve as clearinghouses for the academic job market. Most frequently, each college department is responsible for its own hiring (with the college itself covering the costs), so in addition to placing ads in periodicals, faculty in the departments call colleagues in other schools for recommendations, utilizing every contact at their disposal. Top contenders for positions are then flown to the colleges, where they are interviewed in an intensive and systematic way. They are grilled, primarily of course, by faculty in the departments where the vacancy exists; they are then brought to speak to deans and provosts. Most often, they are required to teach a sample class and to make a formal presentation to faculty and students about their work, their teaching philosophy, and their career expectations. This is an arduous and time-consuming process, but it is only logical that with a tenure system in place, much effort must be invested in finding the right candidate. Colleges recognize that money spent up front means less work and stress in removing an unsuccessful hire.

There is no reason why this process can't be duplicated in public schools around the country. Neither cost nor scheduling can stand in the way. The recruitment of teachers for a teacher-centered school system would include the following:

School systems (usually apprised of vacancies by April 1) would start early in advertising vacancies. Even if a teacher changes her mind about leaving, the benefits of early searching outweigh the liabilities.

School systems would advertise nationally for teaching positions. Ads would be placed in teacher journals and on the Internet (sites already exist for this purpose; they would proliferate if schools took greater advantage of this resource, and costs, which are already minimal, would go down even more). School systems would send teams of teachers each year to such conferences as the National Council for Teachers of English (NCTE) to screen potential candidates and create short lists.

Districts would develop close working relationships with local and regional colleges and university departments of education, tracking promising candidates even before they graduated. Talented college students respond favorably to aggressive recruitment. We have seen many top students choose quite humble districts in which to teach (rejecting the offers of more affluent schools), simply because those districts made them feel special and needed during the interview process. Courting top candidates works, yet few schools take the time to do it.

Teachers would be put front and center in the hiring process. Schools are intimate environments, and to hire a new faculty person without consulting other faculty is like adopting a new child without consulting the other members of the family. No one knows the needs of a department as well as the members of that department. Because hiring is a time-consuming process and not all teachers can be burdened with the task, teacher-centered schools would use their committee structure (see chapter 5) to attend to hiring needs. Teachers elected to hiring committees each year, along with administrators, would be responsible for screening resumes. Administrators would then contact top candidates and arrange interview schedules. When candidates came for interviews, they would meet with hiring committees, administrators, and representatives from the department. Candidates might make presentations after school or teach sample classes to student volunteers.

In districts that are high-need, like rural and inner-city districts, recruitment would be even more rigorous, with more emphasis placed on tracking and courting college undergraduates—the constituency most likely to find such teaching posts challenging and exhilarating. There is an enormous pool of untapped potential in idealistic college students who would prefer urban and inner-city teaching positions, but who often accept offers in suburban districts because those offers come early (the more affluent the district, the more coordinated and prompt its recruitment and hiring) and because they fear nothing else will materialize for them. If urban districts aggressively recruited, they would have far less difficulty attracting good people into their ranks.

SECOND-CAREER PROFESSIONALS

Much has been made in recent years about the importance of attracting second-career professionals to the field. Disgruntled engineers and burned-out lawyers emerge in the popular press as the new saviors of American education, and alternative certification programs are primarily directed to this constituency. Public schools should be grateful, the reasoning goes, that such once–highly paid individuals—individuals smart enough to have passed a bar exam—are now willing to enter so humble a field.

Research on the fate of these second-career teachers suggests that under present circumstances they are struggling mightily to stay afloat.[10] They are most frequently the recipients of alternative licenses, who come to teaching most ill prepared and vulnerable. Plunked down in the toughest schools, with no training and little support, their failure and subsequent exit from the field have consequences apart from the poor schoolchildren who are victims of their incompetence. Many leave teaching even more soured on the state of public education that they were before. They are less likely to vote for bond issues and less likely to place their own children in the public system.

In a teacher-centered school system, there would necessarily be a much smaller need for second-career teachers, as there is no pressing need for second-career lawyers, second-career doctors, or second-career architects. Individuals who truly want to change careers, those who realize that teaching was a missed calling, should be willing to retrain in preparation for that calling. Colleges and universities are replete with evening programs designed to grant certification to adult learners. Such professionals should be sufficiently committed to their new career to spend a semester doing a student teaching internship at the end of their course work. The bottom line is that all teachers should come into the field with a solid background in the subject they will teach and in the science of pedagogy. We ask nothing less of those entering other professions.

RECRUITING RETURNING, RETIRED, AND FOREIGN TEACHERS

If schools were teacher-centered places, fewer teachers would leave or retire early. Those who do, however, should be allowed to return, as long as they can pass state tests to prove that they are still abreast of the knowledge and skills needed for the work. A more interesting pool of talent, however, may be found in foreign teachers, individuals who are English-fluent and who are interested in coming to work and live in the United States. Many states require U.S. citizenship to teach. This requirement was instituted at a time when schools were perceived primarily as centers for cultural assimilation, during the first decades of the last century. But in the twenty-first century, the danger is not pluralism; it is incompetence. The danger is not subversive teaching; it is ignorance and lack of engagement. If schools could expand their applicant pools to include the very best candidates from abroad, that pool would be rich indeed. We have no problem recruiting Indian software engineers, Pakistani doctors, and professional athletes from every country in the world. Bringing to American schools the very best teachers from abroad, and enticing them with quick routes to citizenship and housing perks, would raise the bar on competition for teaching jobs in the most salutary way. Such teachers would have to pass state licensing exams before working, but, once certified, their expertise in sciences and math, foreign language instruction, and computer science would certainly add a level of rigor to many schools. What is more, the diversity of race and ethnicity represented by these foreign teachers would contribute richly to the American public school system.

RETAINING NEW TEACHERS

Statistics suggest that the first three years of teaching are by far the most fraught with difficulty, and that attrition during these years accounts for much of the loss that takes place across the profession.[11] We ourselves have experienced, as teachers in both urban and suburban school districts, the disorientation and stress that comes from sudden immersion in the hectic realities of school life. No preservice program, no matter how exceptional, can remove all of that disorientation, nor can even the best teacher training begin to address the infinite variation of problems and conflicts that teachers face daily.

Teacher-centered schools function, continuously and effectively, as centers of teacher support. Where does a new teacher go when she has a crisis in her classroom? To whom does he speak when he cannot translate the arcane language of a state curricular mandate? Veteran teachers learn strategies that eventually allow them to work fairly autonomously, but new teachers have no such resources. Studies and stories abound that describe the rigors of the first year in the field—the 2 a.m. grading sessions, the pandemonium in the classroom, the remoteness of colleagues and administrators. There is no question that teachers frequently feel lost, helpless, and stressed in their first year on the job. And there is no question that support for such teachers is crucial to retention.[12]

The question is, what kind of support is most useful for new teachers? We believe that the best mentoring for a well-trained, intelligent new teacher should be more psychic than instructive. The assumption in the teacher-centered school is that new teachers know about pedagogy and know their subject. What they do not possess is the basic street savvy of working in the building and the emotional resources to rise above problems and crises. Young teachers need praise. They need constant reminders that their work is meaningful and that it will become easier and more satisfying as time goes on. It is astounding how few new teachers ever receive this kind of stroking. Our experience as teacher educators constantly bears this out: We receive notes each year from recent graduates in which they extol the joys of working with students and rail against the cold, dispassionate attitudes of administrators and fellow teachers. When new teachers complain about the "sink-or-swim" mentality in schools, they are most often not referring to a lack of professional development sessions on how to implement cooperative learning. They are referring to a culture that does not even show them where the fire exits and faculty bathrooms are located.

There are volumes of materials on mentoring first-year teachers, and many states have recently moved to mandate mentoring programs as a requisite for state aid.[13] We are not dismissing the usefulness of some of that literature, but much of the mentoring literature is problematic on a number of levels. First, many mentoring programs assume that a new teacher can be paired with any veteran professional—the designated "mentor"—and that the ensuing relationship will be constructive and supportive. That is not so. New teachers are fragile in very different ways, and some initiative is needed to match the right teacher with the right mentor. Also, many mentoring programs simply create another level of meaningless bureaucracy. When they are state-mandated or designed as prepackaged programs, the apparatus surrounding them is often unnecessarily complex. District mentoring training sessions, mentoring forms, and formal accountability measures seek to enforce mechanically that which could be modestly and quietly done at the school level. If mentoring new recruits becomes another expensive, bureaucratic burden placed on teachers, it defeats the purpose of the work.

Mentoring programs would do well to model themselves on the best programs that currently exist in colleges and universities. Such institutions' strategies for nurturing new teachers are predicated on the idea that the teachers they hire are outstanding to begin with, and the job of the college is to protect the novice's enthusiasm and support creativity. Here are some inexpensive, uncomplicated ways in which this can be done:

Teacher mentoring should be voluntary. Schools could form mentoring committees, composed of teachers who have applied and been chosen by their peers for their ability to do this kind of work successfully. This faculty should be paid well for its service, most of which would be done after school. Mentoring committees would organize lunches and meetings and would monitor, through informal interviews, the changing needs of new teachers. Members of the mentoring committee would also serve as mentors for individual new faculty.

Weekly informal lunches (if the school has a common one-hour lunch period) or weekly after-school teas would provide new and second-year teachers with a predictable and consistent site for support, a place to shop around for a mentor, and a time to meet socially with other new teachers in the school. The problem with many mentoring programs is that the programming is often so infrequent that crises are resolved (poorly or otherwise) long before a mentor can give any input. Standing weekly sessions could be attended by all faculty on the mentoring committee and by any other interested teachers. They should never be mandatory—even for first-year teachers. There should be no set agenda for such get-togethers; young teachers should be encouraged to air their problems without any fear of judgment. The school should pick up the tab for the lunches of anyone who attends (at about three dollars for a cafeteria lunch, that should not break the bank), and nice tea cakes should be served at afternoon sessions. No stale donuts.

Monthly lunchtime or after-school talks by tenured faculty could be scheduled. Again, these should not be mandatory sessions, but informal opportunities for teachers to share with one another examples of best practice or discuss new readings and materials they have found for their classes. At Smith College, we call these liberal arts luncheons. Faculty present "work in progress" in a lively, informal way, while colleagues eat a sandwich. Each month, a faculty committee in charge of coordinating the sessions sends around a list of topics to be presented. It is always astounding to see how many faculty crowd into these sessions. Teachers are genuinely interested in what other teachers are doing, but they have few safe, informal opportunities to share what they know. The much-valued "wisdom of practice" needs a positive, comfortable, and predictable forum in which to be displayed. This kind of professional development is far more valuable than the one-shot input of a consultant who charges the school two thousand dollars for an hour's harangue.

New teachers must be protected as they work to develop rituals and repertoires—as well as the tough skin—needed to survive in the field. This can be done without a career ladder, by simply deciding, as a department, that new teachers get easier assignments. The current strategy of giving new teachers the lowest-level and most difficult classes is cruel and counterproductive. It short-changes the weak students who populate those classes (and who are most desperately in need of veteran professionals), and it drives potentially good teachers out of the field. Currently, schools engage in this practice because there are so few ways to reward good teaching. In a teacher-centered school, where discipline problems would be diminished and where teachers would see themselves as respected and well-compensated professionals, there would be less impulse to "bolt for the brightest." Classes could then be spread evenly around the department, with new teachers spared the hardest assignments: low-level and advanced-placement groups. New teachers should also have as few preparations to perform as possible, allowing them time to adjust to the culture of the school, the demands of the students, and the rhythms of the daily routine.

Teachers need to be given every possible support to succeed. But then they must succeed. And if they do not, or if they are unwilling to work hard at improving their craft, they must not be allowed to stay in the school. In our next chapter, we will speak about teacher evaluation and how, in a teacher-centered school, success is predicated on raising the bar for *everyone* involved in the institution.

NOTES

1. National Commission on Excellence in Education, *A Nation at Risk: The Imperative for Educational Reform: A Report to the Nation and the Secretary* (Washington, D.C.: G. P. O., 1983).

2. Linda Darling-Hammond, "Professional Development for Teachers: Setting the Stage for Learning from Teaching" (Santa Cruz, Calif., 1999), http://www.cftl.org/documents/Darling_Hammond_paper.pdf. See also Ronald F. Ferguson, "Paying for Public Education: New Evidence of How and Why Money Matters," *Harvard Journal on Legislation* 28 (summer 1991): 465–98.

3. Linda Darling-Hammond and Barnett Berry, "Investing in Teaching: Doing What Matters Most for Student Learning," *Commentaries* 4, no. 3 (April 1998):2, http://www.nasbe.org/Educational_Issues/Briefs/Policy_Updates/Teachers/doing.pdf.

4. Mark Fetler, "High School Staff Characteristics and Mathematics Test Results," *Education Policy Analysis Archives* 7, no. 9 (26 March 1999), http://epaa.asu.edu/epaa/v7n9.html.

5. Linda Darling-Hammond, "Teacher Quality and Student Achievement: A Review of State Policy Evidence," *Education Policy Analysis Archives* 8 (January 2000), http://epaa.asu/epaa/v8n1.

6. Natalia Mehlman, "My Brief Teaching Career," *New York Times*, 24 June 2002.

7. U.S. Department of Education, National Center for Education Statistics, htttp://nces.ed.gov/fastfacts/display.asp?id-64.

8. Ibid., http:/nces.ed.gov/fastfacts/display.asp?id-96.

9. Linda Darling-Hammond, Arthur E. Wise, and Stephen P. Klein, *A License to Teach: Raising Standards for Teaching* (San Francisco: Jossey-Bass, 1999); Linda Darling-Hammond, "Who Will Speak for the Children? How Teach for America Hurts Urban Schools and Students," *Phi Delta Kappan* 76, no. 1 (September 1994): 21–34; Linda Darling-Hammond, "How Teacher Education Matters," *Journal of Teacher Education* 51, no. 3 (May 2000): 166–73; Linda Darling-Hammond, "Professional Development for Teachers."

10. G. Natriello and Karen Zumwalt, "Challenges to an Alternative Route to Teacher Certification" in *The Changing Context of Teaching,* ed. Ann Lieberman (Chicago: Chicago University Press, 1992), 59–78. See also Darling-Hammond, Wise, and Klein's powerful critique of Teach for America in *A License to Teach*. See also Darling-Hammond, "Professional Development for Teachers."

11. U.S. Department of Education, National Center for Education Statistics. Twenty-six percent of all new teachers leave the profession after one year and 30 percent within five years. See also Elizabeth F. Fideler and David Haselkorn, *Learning the Ropes: Urban Teacher Induction Practices in the United States* (New York: Recruiting New Teachers, Inc., 1999). The authors discuss the importance of induction programs in retaining teachers in urban schools.

12. Lynn Olson, "Finding and Keeping Competent Teachers," *Education Week* (17 July 2001), http://www.edweek.org. Olson reports that those who do not go through an induction program are twice as likely to give up teaching as those who had support.

13. Craig D. Jerald and Ulrich Boser, "Setting Policies for New Teachers," *Education Week* 19, no. 18 (11 December 2000), http://www.edweek.org/sreports/qc00/templates/article.cfm?slug=policies.htm. See also "Quality Counts 2000:Who Should Teach? Policy Tables: Supporting New Teachers," *Education Week*, http://www.edweek.org/sreports/qc00/tables/ support-t1.htm. The policy tables show that twenty-eight states fund induction programs and nineteen require it.

CHAPTER 5

Tenure and School Governance

In a teacher-centered school, tenure is a critical necessity. Any passing acquaintance with the history of the teaching profession provides ample justification for the perpetuation of tenure laws. Any survey of the voting habits of contemporary American taxpayers reinforces the argument.

As we have discussed, teachers historically have been treated as if they were expendable. Before the rise of unions and the heroic efforts of early activists to gain job security and pensions, teacher exploitation was endemic. Teachers were hired and fired on a whim; communities allowed veteran schoolteachers— spinsters who had served them loyally for forty years—to go to their dotage in penury, without a nickel's worth of support.

In urban areas, teaching positions were assigned through a kind of patronage system, where ward bosses would reward local supporters by granting their daughters positions as schoolteachers. Once the political party was out of favor, those teachers were left unemployed, with no recourse to action. In rural and suburban schools, policies were much the same: Once a teacher was found to be expendable—whether because of her age, her personality, or her political affiliations—she was fired.[1]

Attitudes are no different today. While teachers are now protected by pension and tenure laws, one sees continuous evidence of the risks that would be faced by teachers if those laws were repealed. Too often, communities defeat school bond issues, and even middle-class communities resist maintaining decent working conditions in their public schools. When they are not required by law to paint the building, to raise salaries, or to buy new books for the library, many communities will simply not lay out the money to do so. And when institutions are not bound by contract to retain costly veteran teachers, there is no reason to believe they will. The attack on teacher tenure that has gained such force and adamancy in recent years is motivated, we contend, far less by any professed desire to rid schools of dead wood than by an impulse to cut costs, to reduce budgets by lowering teacher salaries. We have seen a painful example of this in our own community, where a private school, unfettered by tenure laws, summarily dismissed a handful of its most senior faculty when the economy began to weaken.

One reason to retain tenure, then, is to protect communities from their own misguided impulse to save money at the expense of what really counts in schools: quality, experienced teachers, who cost more than inexperienced rookies. A second reason to retain tenure is that it is the one true perquisite of a profession that can provide few others. As the sociologist Dan Lortie has noted, teachers are often, by nature, conservative individuals.[2] The notion of security, of a lifelong job in a predictable environment, is a great draw—more than it might be for lawyers, doctors, and other professionals. For many who choose to teach, the fact of tenure is a critical "benefit" that compensates for other liabilities associated with the work. In a time of teacher shortage, when vacancies have reached crisis proportions, it is counterintuitive to eliminate tenure, the one low-cost lure for good candidates into the profession. A recent study by Harvard University asserts that tenure actually allows schools to maintain less competitive salaries; schools save money as a result of it.[3]

It is easy to see how this is so on the college level, where salaries are considerably lower than in private industry, law, and medicine. Many academics, particularly those in the sciences, could easily be lured to high-paying corporate research jobs. They choose to stay in the academy in part because of the guarantees that go along with employment by such an institution. It is a luxury to remain immune to the vicissitudes of the economy and the rising and falling fortunes of the institution that employs you. It is worth a lower salary for the security of a tenured position. The same is true of the best grade school and high school teachers in America. They too could go elsewhere. Tenure is one good reason to stay.

REFORMING A FLAWED TENURE SYSTEM

As it is currently constituted, however, the public school tenure system simply does not work. American schools are filled with teachers who are weak, disaffected, and incompetent. There are burned-out teachers, poorly educated teachers, and teachers who hate children. These people should never have been allowed to slip through the cracks of the tenure system, burdening schools for the duration of their long careers. No school can successfully transform itself into a teacher-centered institution—into a place where talented, motivated adults feel good about their work — when there exist among their ranks colleagues who are lazy, indifferent, or ignorant. Such people undermine the spirit of schools and drain their colleagues' energy. For the sake of good teachers, bad teachers must be removed.

In most states in the U.S., tenure is granted to a teacher after either two years (in Virginia and Illinois) or three years (in North Carolina, Arkansas, New York, and elsewhere) in the field. The process of obtaining tenure is informal and slipshod. In theory, new teachers should be observed and evaluated in their first years. But because administrators have so little time before tenure automatically "kicks in," and because the high turnover rate crowds schools with untenured teachers, principals and vice-principals are often unable to adequately monitor and assess new faculty. Observations are done hastily, most often by school administrators who are not classroom teachers themselves. Standards for good teaching are amorphous, and criteria for success in the classroom are too often linked only to issues of classroom management. If teachers can keep kids in their seats, they are deemed successful. If they do not molest anybody, they get tenure.

Teacher-centered schools must be predicated on the idea that everyone teaching in that school is a competent, committed professional. To achieve such a high standard among faculty, greater effort must be expended before the tenure process even begins. Teachers' salaries must be raised, the work environment must improve, better strategies for recruiting and hiring must be followed. But once a strong candidate comes into the school, institutions need to devote serious and systematic effort to monitoring and evaluating them. This cannot be done in a rushed and perfunctory way. Nor can it be done only by administrators, whose impressions of a candidate's teaching are limited to observations that are out of context. Untenured teachers need to be assessed in a range of ways and by a range of constituencies. A career-long marriage is at stake: It is reasonable to assume that the prospective partner will be well scrutinized before a formal and lasting commitment is made.

Below, we lay out what we believe to be a meaningful and thorough process for reforming the tenure system in public schools. The reforms are based on four essential changes:

- extending the probationary period for teachers from three to six years
- requiring an advanced degree
- requiring a portfolio and/or other forms of concrete documentation of a teacher's growth
- requiring extensive observations and assessments by teachers, administrators, and community members

Extending the Probationary Period

In colleges and universities, the pre-tenure period for faculty is six years; such an extended probationary term makes good sense, for a number of reasons. First, it affords new teachers time to settle in before they are rigorously assessed. Academic faculty often spend the first year or two getting oriented in their institution, establishing their courses and the teaching strategies that work best, and finding a niche in the school community. Their value as teachers and scholars cannot be assessed during this settling-in period. A six-year probationary term gives the school and the department a chance to get to know faculty members, not in their frantic first years, but as they will be as real colleagues, after they have had a chance to settle in. Six years is enough time to know if colleagues are team players, if they are flexible, affable, capable of taking on responsibilities apart from what is required of them. It also allows a chance for leisurely, thoughtful evaluations of the teacher's classroom performance, the key factor determining the viability of a candidate.

An extended probationary period also gives the granting of tenure real weight and value. In the academic world, tenure is a significant rite of passage, a major milestone in a teacher's career. Successful tenure decisions are treated as joyous events—as meaningful and important as the publishing of a first book or the attaining of an advanced degree. We believe that tenure in the teacher-centered school can and should take on this same weight and significance.

Requiring an Advanced Degree

It is not unreasonable to assume that teachers elevated into tenured status would hold a master's degree, or other appropriate advanced degree, in their subject field. Given that a successful tenure decision would be accompanied by a significant raise—10 percent, not including cost-of-living increases—it is right that such teachers have credentials that extend beyond the minimum ones required for employment. A master's degree, master of arts in teaching, master of fine arts, and master in education degrees may all offer a teacher the appropriate expertise warranted for a tenured status in the profession. We do believe, however, that schools should be allowed to maintain flexibility in the kinds of degrees they will accept for tenure. An English teacher we know in Connecticut (a state that currently requires for permanent certification a master's degree "in the subject taught") was forced to leave his position because he possessed a Ph.D. in comparative literature, not English. This kind of absurd bureaucratic regulation is exactly what teacher-centered schools would be allowed to avoid. An M.B.A. should not count toward tenure in French, but it might well be acceptable for a position in math. It should be up to the discretion of the school to decide.

Requiring a Portfolio and Other Documentation

As longtime teachers, we have often marveled at the misguided notion that student improvement can be accurately assessed by standardized tests. It has always seemed obvious that an outsider who wished to gauge the real progress of students need only look at sample work from the beginning of the year and the end of the year. The difference between the two is the measure of the teacher's success—a concrete manifestation of his labor and commitment.

This is the principle behind the tenure portfolio. When, in their sixth year, teachers come up for tenure, they should be required to submit a body of work that documents their six years of employment. Again, this is standard practice in colleges and universities, where the tenure process proceeds something like this: Academic faculty submit portfolios of course syllabi and pertinent teaching materials, published and unpublished articles and books, and letters and other forms of written support. These materials are reviewed by the candidate's department, by a college-level committee of peers (often called the committee on tenure and promotion), and by outside, unbiased experts in the field. The views of all three of these bodies are weighed and considered by the provost, the president, and ultimately by the board of trustees, who have the final say in the fate of the candidate.

On the public school level, much the same process might easily be followed, though the content of the portfolio would necessarily differ. Teachers would submit portfolios of their best work: lesson and unit plans, rubrics, assignments, tests, and samples of student work. They would include documentation of courses taken and workshops attended, service rendered to the school or department, and articles written. Also included might be letters of testimony from former students, from parents, and from colleagues. Most important, teachers would have to write self-evaluations, describing their growth over time and explaining their philosophy of teaching. Portfolios would be compiled slowly; they would become a clearly visible record of the six years spent in the school.

Two copies of these portfolios would be submitted at the start of the sixth year, the tenure year. Held in both the principal's office and the central office of the board of education, they would be available for several weeks for public scrutiny—by other teachers in the school, by parents, and by members of the larger community. Lists of the names of teachers who were coming up for tenure in any given year might be catalogued in the local paper each September. The public would be invited to respond in writing to the work of the candidates and to send testimony of a child's positive or negative experiences in a teacher's classroom. These letters would be added to the teacher's portfolio and would be a rich source of data for making the decision.

Requiring Extensive Community Assessment

Because teaching is a performance activity, and because it is the cornerstone of the teacher's job, those who evaluate the fate of pretenure teachers must have intimate and ongoing knowledge of that teacher's ability in front of a classroom. In most schools, teacher observation and assessment is uneven, to say the least. Most teachers are observed solely by administrators, who often come and go in the classroom, spending only the briefest time there, and whose view of good teaching may differ from the view of the teacher in question and from that of other teachers in the school. Since administrators are necessarily concerned, in their own jobs, with issues of management and control, they tend to focus on these in their assessments. If students are well behaved, if they remain in their seats and respond to adult authority, the teacher is deemed successful. New teachers know that the key to achieving status in an administrator's eyes is to avoid ever sending a student to the office.

In teacher-centered schools, where principals are engaged in the work of teaching, their ability to assess good pedagogy would necessarily be more sophisticated and complex. But that is not enough. Schools need to develop, through long and thoughtful discussions that involve all the various constituencies in the building, a series of general principles about what it means to teach well. Such discussions are tantamount to developing a philosophy of education, a shared system of beliefs that can be articulated by all concerned—students, teachers, and those who work in the cafeteria. In outstanding schools—particularly private schools—discussions of teaching philosophy are seen not as a waste of time but as a necessity for survival. A private school needs to sell itself to the community, to distinguish itself from other institutions offering comparable services. One might say of the Calhoun School, in New York, "That is a progressive school, with a creative, experientially based curriculum." Of Collegiate, in the same city, one might say, "That is a traditional school, where subjects are taught in more traditional ways." Teachers choose to work in one school over another based as much on their own teaching styles as on any other factor.

In a public school, of course, there needs to be much greater latitude in the definition of what constitutes good teaching. The philosophy of a public school must be broad enough to encompass the beliefs of a very wide constituency. Public schools, which serve the needs of diverse students, could not and should not insist on one style of pedagogy. But within loose parameters, there can still be consensus about general principles of good teaching, and there is always a need for ongoing debate and reassessment of an institution's values. When teachers and administrators go into the classrooms of novice teachers, they should be looking for an agreed-upon set of criteria for judging excellence.

It is not difficult to find intelligent examples of such broad criteria for best practice in the burgeoning materials issued by such groups as the National Council of Teachers of Science[4] or the National Board of Professional Teaching Standards.[5] The latter, for example, has published what it calls "five core propositions" about excellent teaching, standards used to judge candidates for National Board certification. In brief, these general principles reflect an accepted view of good teaching that is neither confining nor ideological:

1. Teachers are committed to students and their learning. They recognize individual differences, they adjust their practices based on observation and reflection, they apply theories of cognition and theories of intelligence to their practice.

2. Teachers know the subjects they teach and how to teach those subjects. Teachers are expert in their fields and know how to translate their complex understanding of a subject to children. Their instructional repertoire is broad.

3. Teachers are responsible for managing and monitoring student learning: They know how to hold the interest of children, how to manage small groups and large ones, how to motivate students, how to measure student growth and learning, and how to clearly explain student performance to parents.

4. Teachers think systematically about their practice and learn from experience: Accomplished teachers are models of educated persons. Their decisions in the classroom are grounded in both research and in experience; they are self-critical and reflective.

5. Teachers are members of learning communities. They are capable of working collaboratively on developing curriculum and instructional policies. They understand the state and local objectives and work to address them; they are receptive to parents.

Lists like this one, developed through thoughtful discussion, serve as useful rubrics for separating the acceptable from the unacceptable. Observers of classrooms in a teacher-centered school should know the criteria by which they are assessing what they see.

What is more, observation and evaluation of teaching must be done by a much broader constituency than is currently involved in this work. New teachers need to be observed systematically by department chairs and by other teachers in the school, and these observations need to be documented with narrative reports that give a clear sense of the work under scrutiny. By the time teachers reach the point of tenure, their work in the classroom should be well known, their strengths and weaknesses as teachers formally recorded.

If this rigorous screening process were adopted, schools would let go a significant number of teachers long before their sixth year of employment. Those who make it to the sixth year and are denied tenure should not be allowed to remain in the school. While colleges often give unsuccessful candidates one additional year for job-hunting, we do not believe public schools are obliged to do the same. A teacher who does not receive tenure should know of the school's decision by the early spring, which would give sufficient time to apply elsewhere for work. The point is to get rid of anyone who is not excellent at what they do and to do it as quickly as possible.

POST TENURE

The years directly after tenure, the midcareer period in a teacher's life, are potentially years of high productivity. Teachers at this point are still vital enough to make energetic contributions to the school. They also possess the "wisdom of practice," that particular kind of teacher knowledge that comes only from rich experience.[6] Teacher-centered schools recognize that if they can keep this valuable constituency in the school through the tenth or twelfth year, they will likely retain them for life.

How does one continue to reward and nurture the midcareer teacher? Policy makers in the 1980s and 1990s tended to favor the career ladder as the most viable strategy for maintaining incentive in this cohort: Set up a system of promotion, the reasoning went, wherein teachers could rise up the ranks like corporate executives. Each step of the ladder would be accompanied by a raise, a new title, and a slightly altered job description. The master teacher, the most senior and august level, would have less teaching and more administrative duties, including teacher assessment and curriculum work.

In theory, the notion of a career ladder makes some sense. Teachers, like everyone else, need to feel that hard work and persistence will be rewarded. But experiences with career ladders around the country suggest that they are almost impossible to implement fairly. Career ladders tend to undermine teacher collegiality—a school's most precious commodity. Teachers wonder whether decisions for promotion are political, or they sense they must compete against one another for limited resources. In Texas, career ladders foundered when districts began changing the criteria for achieving the status of master teacher—upping the ante for promotion—when funds to support those teachers dwindled.[7] The gains of such a system are not worth the liabilities.

Truly meaningful compensation after tenure would acknowledge and celebrate tenured teachers as committed, intellectual professionals. These rewards should be designed to take advantage of the strengths of this cohort—their expertise in curriculum and in pedagogy—while preserving morale and collegiality. Here are some suggestions of how to do that:

1. Involve midcareer and veteran teachers in the running of the school.

A teacher-centered school must be built around a democratic system of governance, wherein veteran professionals are allowed to assume responsibility for their practice. In such a school, teachers at any point in their careers, but most certainly after tenure, would be encouraged to participate on formal governance committees that define school policy, support novice teachers, and make key decisions about hiring and firing. For some of these services, they must be paid; others can be voluntary. No teacher should be obligated to do this work every year. But the option for compensated, meaningful committee work must exist in the school. Some teachers will rarely take advantage of it; some will do so frequently. The school only stands to gain from those who do.

The structure of governance that we propose here follows the one employed by many small liberal arts colleges. There, faculty and administration work closely, overlapping domains in ways that foster mutual respect. Faculty make policy decisions; administrators teach. The lines of power become blurred in the process. This system of governance is cost-efficient, because it enables a school system to hire fewer administrators. But more importantly a democratic system of governance serves to renew and energize faculty, to give them opportunities to embrace new kinds of challenges and think in new ways about their field. It is an excellent form of professional development.

While every school would adapt its own particular governance structure, the following list suggests some of the committees necessary for running a teacher-centered school:

Faculty Council

Colleges are often run by a faculty council or senate, which advises the president and board of trustees on issues of broad concern to the school. The committee's main function is to serve as a kind of overseer for all other committees at the school and to develop, along with the administration, the larger mission and priorities of the college. Faculty members who serve on this important and time-consuming committee often receive compensation in the form of a course release or stipend. For a teacher-centered school, we propose a similar kind of committee, elected by faculty, which would work with the principal and vice-principal in similar ways. The committee would send individual representatives to each of the other committees in the school, would function as the voice of the faculty in all matters involving the administration, and would serve as a sounding board for all staff as they implement new policy or curricular initiatives. Faculty serving on this committee would receive a course release.

Mentoring Committee

This group of the most distinguished and veteran teachers in the school would be chosen to serve on a rotating basis to work with new teachers and help them during the first two years of their employment in the school. The group would be responsible for helping teachers in all areas of their work—acclimating them to school procedures, record keeping, learning the school culture, and classroom instruction and management. Mentors would work one-on-one with novices and meet regularly with untenured faculty as a whole, offering lectures and informal support sessions. Members of the mentoring committee must be well compensated for their work. A salary supplement of two to three thousand dollars for the work is not unreasonable in a middle-class district.

Hiring Committee

This rotating group of faculty would be responsible for helping the principal identify hiring needs, frame advertisements for openings, recruit candidates, and conduct interviews for all academic positions throughout the school. When choosing the final candidate, the hiring committee would most often defer to the opinion of the individual department undergoing the search, but the committee might also function to break a deadlock between two candidates. Members of the hiring committee should also receive substantial compensation.

Tenure and Retention Committee

This committee would be responsible for making critical decisions about the tenure and/or retention of teachers in the school. Composed of the school's most senior and respected faculty, the committee would review all tenure portfolios, would observe the teaching of faculty who were up for tenure, and would make final recommendations to the board of education. In the case of teachers whose work has been deemed problematic, the committee would help departments and administrators build their case for retention or dismissal by making additional observations and coaching weak teachers. Teachers serving on this committee would receive a course release.

Disciplinary Committee

This committee would review cases of students petitioning for reentry after suspensions, expulsions, and terms in alternative high schools. The committee would meet on an as-needed basis and would be voluntary.

2. Utilize midcareer and veteran teachers to develop the curriculum during the summer.

The idea that a person who has never taught or who last taught many years ago would be in charge of developing curriculum for students is illogical. Curriculum should be developed by talented, experienced classroom teachers, who know the real needs and capacities of students and who are most invested in the materials that are developed. If rotating teams of the district's strongest teachers were paid well to collaboratively refine and revise the school's curriculum on a yearly basis, the district would end up benefiting in a number of ways. First, they would save a significant amount of money. If ten teachers a year were paid $4,000 for curriculum summer work, the combined expense would be considerably less than the average income of a single district curriculum coordinator. Second, the task would benefit from the wisdom and expertise of ten talented professionals instead of one. Finally, the curriculum would be fad-free, clear, and easy to implement. It is unlikely that a veteran teacher would accept materials or strategies that seem illogical, pretentious, or trendy. Using tenured teachers for summer curriculum work would also afford those teachers the additional income many would otherwise earn by painting houses or doing other menial work that leaves teachers more tired in September than they were in June.

Teacher-driven curriculum work can only be meaningful, however, if schools are not driven by standardized and high-stakes tests. Boatloads of invective have been directed against these tests and their harmful influence on children.[8] Less has been written about their effects on teachers. Quite simply, such tests are poison for teacher-centered schools. They demoralize teachers; they rout out creativity in pedagogy; they drive the best and brightest out of the field. What talented person would want to stay in a profession where work is scripted and where her best efforts are reduced to a bottom-line score, publicized in the local paper, which represented no real measure of the growth of her students or the complex labor in which she engaged? The fraudulence and waste surrounding the testing movement is a bitter subject for teachers. Many have seen bright students who fail tests because their strengths cannot be measured in simplistic ways; many have also seen colleagues produce high pass rates by drumming formulas into their students' heads.

High-stakes tests, and the mushrooming materials that attend them, must be eliminated for teacher-centered schools to take hold. Advocates of such tests need only listen to the best teachers in the country to know they are on the wrong track.[9] As long as they choose not to listen, schools will not improve.

3. Rethink professional development.

Some of the most respected scholars in the field of education believe in the efficacy of professional development and write with conviction that good in-service training can make all the difference for teachers.[10] But, given the common experience of most teachers in America, it is sometimes hard to believe it. Perhaps no other aspect of the teacher's job is so maligned and mocked as in-service training. Virtually every teacher in America can offer stories of inane workshops that tried his patience to the limit: inspirational speakers who harangue teachers about positive thinking; stress-reduction experts who ask teachers to lie on the floor and pretend they are crustaceans; writing consultants who ask teachers to describe a cookie in prose or write poems about their pets. In response, teachers knit, or surreptitiously grade papers, or pass bawdy notes to one another. Mainly, they feel resentful.

The problem with most professional development, from a teacher's perspective, is that it fails to account for the complex and various needs of real teachers. Consultants may instruct teachers in principles of multiple intelligence and "readiness to learn," but such generic workshops by their very nature contradict the principles they espouse. At any moment in the life of a faculty, concerns and weaknesses, interests and skills vary enormously. Rarely will one topic be useful to all faculty at the same time.

Teachers are also keenly aware of the expense of outside consultants, which prejudices them against the messages such visitors impart. A single speaker with a national reputation can use up one-third of a school's yearly budget for teacher training. Given their own modest wages, the exorbitant cost of a one-hour performance cannot help but rankle. It just does not seem like the best use of limited resources.

In a teacher-centered school, in-service training would play an integral role, but it would be tailored to teachers' individual needs and would be respectful of their individual talents in ways rarely practiced today. Let the following four principles guide professional development in the teacher-centered school:

a. Most formal professional development in a school should be created and led by teachers themselves. In schools that have recruited and nurtured skilled professionals, the contributions of those veterans are far more valuable than the input of outsiders. Teachers in public schools are rarely asked to conduct their own in-service programming. This is a terrible waste of talent. Teachers should be invited to present other faculty with personal strategies, pedagogies, and skills gleaned from their own rich experience, and they should be paid well for this work.

b. All professional development workshops should be optional. In colleges, rich programming is constantly being offered, and faculty choose to attend or not, based on personal interest in the subject presented. Schools must have enough respect for the integrity of teachers to allow them to decide for themselves. Offering a variety of sessions on a range of topics acknowledges the individual differences between teachers and virtually guarantees that when teachers do choose to come, they will pay attention.

c. Teachers should be encouraged and supported to observe one another's classes. No in-service training is as meaningful as watching a great practitioner model an outstanding lesson. This is why student teaching is the most useful part of teacher education: We learn best by example. In a school that is rich with excellent teachers, there is much to be learned by simply watching one another. For this to happen, administrators must budget funds for substitutes and must be willing to fill in for teachers at short notice. Allowing for these observations—indeed, encouraging them—needs to be a priority for administrators.

d. Encourage continuous, individualized professional development through conferences and workshops outside the school. Most of the professional development budget should be directed to travel and fees associated with subject-specific development. Teachers should be encouraged to attend learned society meetings in their disciplines, meetings of the National Council of Teachers of Math or English, or National Endowment for the Humanities (NEH) seminars especially designed for schoolteachers. These sessions are often excellent clearinghouses for new ideas in the field. Annual conferences offer a wide smorgasbord of ideas, and attending such meetings serves to reinforce the sense of teachers as professionals, as scholars of their discipline or of pedagogy itself. Administrators should work hard to match teachers with conferences and workshops that occur regionally and suggest (without pressure) that attendance might be interesting and helpful.

The general principle guiding all professional development, whether in the school or outside it, whether teacher-led or consultant-driven, is that it must respect the individual needs and individual interests of teachers. One size simply cannot fit all.

4. Offer sabbaticals.

The notion of a sabbatical, a paid period of leave in which a scholar can pursue scholarly ideas, stands as a key characteristic of intellectual teaching. Good colleges, of course, build large numbers of sabbaticals into yearly budgets. Many private schools also offer sabbatical leaves to faculty members on a competitive basis. Budgeting for 1 percent of tenured faculty to pursue a sabbatical leave each year would not bankrupt any school system, and knowing that such a leave exists would have a salutary effect on faculty. Sabbaticals would allow veteran teachers to think in terms of ambitious, scholarly projects and would encourage them to develop proposals for new classes or to outline for themselves lists of new readings they want to do—not only to enrich the curriculum, but also for their own personal growth. For many years, the NEH has offered summer stipends for teachers to study literary or historical topics presented by college or university faculty. Teachers who take these seminars return to their classes energized and stimulated.[11] The same good would emerge from the semester-long sabbatical at full pay or a yearlong sabbatical at two-thirds salary.

The fact that few sabbaticals could be offered in any given year would not necessarily create intense competition for these leaves. Many teachers would not want to leave teaching for a year of independent study. When more applications are received than can be accommodated, teachers would simply defer to a principle of seniority. If a teacher's proposal was good, she would know that eventually it would be supported.

In general, tenured teachers in teacher-centered schools will want to stay in their positions because their salaries are good, their jobs are secure, their working conditions are excellent, their colleagues are bright and stimulating, and they love to teach. Add to that the options for sabbaticals, summer work, meaningful input in governance, and rich professional development, and the turnover rate, we contend, will be very small indeed.

REMOVING BAD TENURED TEACHERS

At present, the only way a school can be rid of a bad tenured teacher is if that teacher commits some kind of grievous act. A lazy teacher, an ignorant teacher, a boring and abusive teacher who has made it through the tenure process can retain a position in a school for life. This is an untenable situation. Teachers who are classified as "dead wood" are not only a burden to students, they are a double burden to their colleagues, a poison in the work environment, and a source of demoralization.

In teacher-centered schools, the assumption is that such teachers will be almost nonexistent. If faculty are well trained and rigorously recruited, if they are mentored and carefully evaluated before tenure, and if they are stimulated after tenure with new challenges, the chances of conventional burnout will be much diminished. There will be instances, however, when an incompetent teacher does slip through the cracks or a once-good teacher simply stops doing a good job. In such cases, schools must be vigilant about documenting the incompetence and pursuing the teacher's dismissal with aggressive energy. What is more, teachers themselves must become more involved in this process. If a teacher-centered school is to thrive, the overall good of the school must outweigh arcane codes of loyalty. Both the American Federation of Teachers and the National Educational Association support peer review and assistance programs, wherein teachers counsel and support colleagues whose work is below par.[12] In a teacher-centered school, the committee on tenure and retention would do this work. If prolonged and earnest effort produce no positive result, these teachers would join with administrators and parents in documenting the incompetence and campaigning for the teacher's removal.

NOTES

1. Nancy Hoffman, *Woman's True Profession* (Old Westbury, N.Y.: Feminist Press, 1981).

2. Dan Lortie, *School Teacher: A Sociological Study* (Chicago: University of Chicago Press, 1977), 1–24.

3. See Cathy A. Trower, "Can Colleges Competitively Recruit Faculty without the Prospect of Tenure?" in *The Questions of Tenure,* ed. Richard P. Chait (Cambridge: Harvard University Press, 2002). Trower writes, "Without tenure, institutions of lesser prestige could not afford to match salaries that would be required to attract and retain able faculty" (p. 182).

4. National Science Education Standards, http://www.nap.edu/read ingroom/books/nses/html/3.html.

5. National Board of Professional Teaching Standards, http://www .nbpts.org.

6. Lee Shulman, "Knowledge and Teaching: Foundations of the New Reform," *Harvard Educational Review* 57, no. 1 (February 1987): 1–22.

7. Glyn D. Ligon, "Data Quality: Earning the Confidence of Decision Makers," (paper presented at the annual meeting of the American Educational Research Association, New York, April 1996), http://www.educationadvisor.com/ocio2001/DATAQUAL.DOC_. Ligon writes, "When Texas implemented a career ladder for teachers, we had to certify those eligible based upon their annual evaluations. The school board determined that they were going to spend only the money provided by the State for career ladder bonuses, so that set the maximum number of teachers who could be placed on the career ladder." See also "Teacher Salaries and State Priorities: A Vital Link," Educational Benchmark 2000, http://www.sreb.org/main/Benchmarks2000/Teacher. The report is highly critical of career ladders that were put into place in Texas and around the country in the 1980s: "While the cost of fully implementing the programs became a budget issue, the controversies over the perceived fairness of incentives based on evaluations were the reason for the eventual elimination of the programs" (p. 9).

8. Greg Winter, "More Schools Rely on Tests but Study Raises Doubts," *New York Times*, 28 December 2002. This front-page article reported on results of the largest national study ever undertaken of high-stakes tests, their impact and efficacy. Researchers found that states that mandated high-stakes tests had uniformly higher dropout rates. They also found that students in these states consistently performed more poorly on other national comparative measures, including SAT and ACT tests. Researchers explained the attrition and poor performance in these states by concluding that the make-or-break nature of the exams forced teachers to ignore students' individual needs and to focus on test preparation at the expense of other vital areas of the curriculum.

9. Dale Johnson and Bonnie Johnson, "The Unfairness of Uniformity," *Reading Today* (August/September 2002): 18, http://www.reading.org/publications/rty/02aug_unfair.html. The Johnsons' experience in rural Louisiana summarizes and synthesizes, in vivid detail, the complaints that many teachers level against high-stakes testing. The Johnsons, both academics, decided to spend a year back in the elementary classroom. They relocated to rural Louisiana, to a community composed mainly of African American children. They found the following conditions in their school: "The school has no library, no playground

equipment, no hot water for washing hands, no art teacher, no counselor, and one toilet for seventy-two faculty and staff. We began our year with no maps, one globe between us, a shortage of textbooks, dictionaries from 1952, malfunctioning heating/cooling systems, and a healthy supply of cockroaches and other pests." Louisiana, the authors write, has "fallen under the spell" of high-stakes testing: "Children in fourth and eighth grade must pass the state exam or they fail the grade. They may retake the test after attending summer school, but if they fail it twice, they must repeat the grade. The children we taught are as bright as any with whom we have worked. In an era of high-stakes tests, however, they are viewed without compassion. . . . many of the children came to school sick and remained there all day—not because the mother didn't care, but because the mother was afraid to miss a day of work. . . . our pupils were lacking in the kinds of prior knowledge required for adequate test performance. . . . must had never traveled any farther than to a Wal-Mart that was 20 miles away. . . . Our students could sound out unfamiliar words such as 'harp,' 'opera,' or 'waitress,' but they were unable to map the sounds onto any meaning, never having been to a restaurant with a waitress, nor ever having heard opera. Since such a high number of the students failed the test, the school was labeled 'academically below average.' No attempts were made to supply the school with extra books or resources. Rather, the state's solution was to threaten with eventual closure if the school doesn't start 'performing.'"

10. Linda Darling-Hammond, in many of the articles and books cited in these notes, builds a strong, intelligent case for the value of professional development. A problem remains, however, in how schools implement and interpret her recommendations. In his article "Creating a Knowledge Base for Teaching," *Educational Leadership* 59, no. 6 (March 2002): 6, Willis Scott says, "professional development should be targeted and directly related to teacher's practice. It should be site-based and long-term. It should be ongoing—part of a teacher's work week. And it should be curriculum-based, to the extent possible, so that it helps teachers help their students master the curriculum at a higher level." See also James W. Stigler and James Hiebert, *The Teaching Gap: Best Ideas from the World's Teachers for Improving Education* (New York: Free Press, 1999).

11. National Humanities Alliance, testimony on the FY2002 appropriations for the National Endowments of the Humanities, presented to the Interior and Related Agencies Subcommittee of the House Appro-

priations Committee, http://www.nhalliance.org. Each year, NEH receives enthusiastic feedback from teachers around the country who completed seminars and institutes over the summer. The following are some examples of comments received by NEH from teacher participants in the 2000 summer seminars and institutes: "Upon my return to the classroom, I was able to immediately put into practice knowledge and skills learned during the seminar." "My sense of the importance of teaching the humanities has been renewed, and I am more zealous than ever about the role that they should play in everyone's life."

12. Eileen Mary Weis and Stephen Gary, "New Directions in Teacher Evaluation," Office of Educational Research and Improvement, December 2000, ERIC, ED 429052. The authors report: "American Federation of Teachers and National Education Association locals have initiated peer review and assistance programs in districts such as Rochester, New York; Toledo, Columbus, and Cincinnati, Ohio; and Seattle, Washington (Career in Teaching Joint Governing Panel, 1996; Columbus Education Association, 1997; NCTAF, 1996; Toledo Federation of Teachers, 1996). Because these systems rely on teachers having increased opportunities for decision-making and collaboration with colleagues, the process of evaluation becomes an integral part of everyday practice. Altering the process by which teachers are evaluated is providing the impetus for deeper structural changes in their responsibilities. For example, through a rigorous process, a governing panel of teachers and administrators selects consulting teachers who mentor untenured teachers and intervene with tenured teachers having difficulty. Along with increased autonomy comes greater accountability. In each program, standards have been strengthened for obtaining tenure and remaining in teaching."

CHAPTER 6

A Utopian Vision: Case Study of William Dewey

When William Frost Dewey first graduated from high school, he was sure he was going to be a famous writer. He loved to write and he loved to read, especially the long nineteenth-century novels that had allowed him to escape the mundane realities of life in an east coast suburb. William was a scholar, one of only a handful of kids in his high school who really got pleasure out of hard intellectual labor. He took every advanced class his large regional high school had to offer. He spent his summers first as a student, and then as a teaching assistant at a nearby private school which offered summer enrichment classes in the arts and humanities. "I was insatiable! I couldn't get enough of being a student," he says. "During those summers I used to sit with a group of like-minded kids—geeks like me—and read poetry out loud under the stars."

As William Dewey speaks now, he nervously weaves a yellow number-two pencil in and out of his fingers. He is a tall, dark-haired man of forty-five, broadly built but with a slight scholarly stoop. He is wearing a worn tweed jacket, a nice tie, and a pair of chinos. His face is intense and there is a slightly abstracted manner about him, as if he has spent many years being interrupted and has found a way to retreat into privacy even in the presence of other people.

"It was not until I got to Swarthmore," William explains, "that I ever thought about becoming a teacher. One day during my sophomore year I was lolling around in the English department, and the chair of the department—I had her for Chaucer—came up to me and said, 'Will, you know you're a born teacher.' I guess she'd seen the way I went wild over the passages we'd discuss in seminar. She saw my enthusiasm. Anyway, the minute she said it, something clicked in me, and I thought, 'Of course! A teacher! Absolutely!' and then I thought, 'But am I smart enough?'"

William enrolled in the teacher education sequence at Swarthmore, a series of seven courses that culminated in state certification. The courses were difficult and interesting. William studied child development with one of the foremost scholars in that field. He worked one-on-one with autistic and deaf children through a course on disabilities. He read the works of Rousseau, Locke, Mill, and William James in a class on educational philosophy and spent a full semester poring over the challenging writing of John Dewey in a class that forever changed the way he thought about himself as a learner, a citizen, and an individual.

During the fall of his senior year, William team-taught in the local high school, two tenth-grade classes in American literature and a class on basic writing skills for a group of developmentally disabled freshmen. During his internship, he helped teachers design curriculum, met regularly with parents, and even trailed the principal for a day, slowly developing a sense of how good schools run. He worked with two strong veteran teachers, both of whom encouraged him and pressed him hard at the same time. "Student teaching was the most difficult, intellectually challenging thing I'd ever done in my life," Will says. "Putting theory into practice. Juggling all those personalities and demands. I used to come home from school each day drenched in sweat, and think, 'God, this is incredible. This is such a privilege!'"

During his senior year, Will received a phone call from a principal in Cincinnati. Russ Miller was a Swarthmore graduate himself and, as he explained on the phone, had kept up a close relationship with the department of education. He was scouting recruits for his school, he said, and had been given Will's name and number by the chair of the education department. "Russ said I came highly recommended! Needless to say, I was really flattered," Will says, "I was, like, Sign me up!" During January term, Will took the train to Cincinnati. "Even twenty-odd years later, I remember that day. It was so pivotal." The school had paid for Will's transportation and lodging in the city, and he recalls that when he disembarked into the station, a trio of teachers was waiting to pick him up. "The English chair, the chair of the hiring committee, and a young recruit from the year before—my future best friend—Allen Able. They were all standing there smiling, and I thought: This is looking good! Little did I know what I was in for!"

Will describes the interview process as "grueling." "Six hours straight of interviews, tours, teaching, schmoozing. First I met with the department chair, Elizabeth Ames; then with the principal; then with the hiring committee; then I taught a Yeats poem to an eleventh-grade class; then I gave a talk about my senior essay research; then I met again with the department." By the end of the day, Will was certain that he wanted to teach in Clifton High School. But he was not so certain that they wanted him. "All along I kept thinking, why me? Everyone wants to teach in a school like this. It's a dream job. Why should they choose someone without a master's degree? Someone who can't coach a sport?" Later, Russ Miller would tell Will that though forty applicants had applied for the job, it was clear to everyone that he was the right candidate. "We were looking for brains and spirit," Russ says. "We saw in Will's enthusiasm and love of learning the kind of person we could work with, the kind of person who we could help to become a real master teacher."

Will moved to Cincinnati in the summer, right after graduation. He immediately took the Ohio certification test and, armed with his English major and certification in Pennsylvania, was quickly granted a reciprocal license. The school had helped him relocate, finding him an apartment and subsidizing the move. "From the point of view of a college student, I was being paid a princely wage. They started me off at $42,000, and I went out and bought all the things I had never been able to afford: a good stereo, a bedroom set, the complete works of Shakespeare in separate volumes. I began my first day of my first year in the first good sports jacket I'd ever bought. I wanted to look respectable, professional. I hadn't even started to teach yet, and I already felt gratitude to this school."

Will remembers his first year as if it were yesterday. Even with the strong training he'd received at Swarthmore, the work was still challenging. Assigned three classes of upper-level sophomores and one eleventh grade world literature class with a total enrollment of seventy-eight, Will felt compelled to work long into the night, developing strategies for motivating his bright students. "I had all these lessons and unit plans and materials that the department had given me. And still I was at sea. I thought, this stuff is great and I'll use some of it, but I really need to make my own, to make it mine." Will says the support he received early on from his chair and from members of the mentoring committee was what kept him afloat. "Every Friday afternoon I would meet in the lounge with the four other new teachers and the mentoring committee, and it was like a free-for-all. There would be so many questions and wild stories, and we would laugh about the stupidest things that people had done. I looked forward to those sessions with such anticipation. It was so easy-going; there was no judgement. And, God! I got such good advice!"

It was at one of these Friday sessions that Will met his mentor, Paula Rosen, a fourteen-year veteran history teacher with a sly, ironic manner that immediately put Will at ease. "I needed to be mentored by someone tough, someone who could take a joke," Will says. Paula began to visit Will's classes every other week, taking notes and debriefing with him on the phone in the evening. "The sessions were the most meaningful professional development I've ever received. It was amazing. Like a young actor getting a biweekly critique from Al Pacino. Paula spoke to me about everything: my body language, my projection, how I framed my questions, how I spoke to boys differently from girls. It was a revelation." Now retired, Paula remains a close friend. "She was my life raft, and I'll never be able to thank her enough," he says.

Will was also helped in his first year by Russ Miller, who punctuated his work as principal with frequent teaching. Every other year, Russ offered an elective in one of the many areas of social studies he enjoyed. He had taught classes in civics and psychology, in medical ethics and international relations. Teachers often commented that Russ's interests were so wide and various, and his people skills so refined, that he might well have gone into investigative journalism. Indeed, Will says, Russ had a way of drawing out the best in people—both students and faculty—and getting them to reveal sides of themselves they didn't even know existed. He'd certainly done this for Will. In the first months of school, Will observed Russ teaching an introduction to law class and had been so impressed with the complex debate structure that the principal had used there that he decided to replicate it in his own classes. The strategy proved highly successful and became a permanent part of Will's teaching repertoire.

Russ was also responsible for connecting Will to the Poets and Writers Collaborative in Cincinnati, where he found a support group for his own fiction, and also to the teacher workshop sessions offered in the summer. Russ, working with the school's professional development committee, seemed positively obsessed with matching young teachers to programs and conferences that fit their individual interests. "I loved Russ, and so did everyone else," Will says. "He was the heart and soul of the school, wise and caring." When Russ died, several years ago, after many years in retirement, teachers who still loved him contributed money to build a gazebo outside the school, bearing his name.

It is in that gazebo that we are now sitting, on a cool September day. The school itself rises in front of us, a square brick building of modest size with large windows and a wide, terraced front yard. Spanning the terraces are a series of broad garden beds, filled with flowers, vegetables, and herbs. Small groups of students take turns tending the gardens, the fruits of which service the cafeteria. "It was my friend Allen's idea," Will explains. "He had a garden at home and he knew how satisfying it was to make things grow. Kids line up to get on garden duty. Some of the roughest kids, the ones who have the hardest time reading *Beowulf,* thrive when they get outside." We look together at the rows of zucchinis and tomatoes and at the half-dozen kids weeding around them. "Hey, Mr. D," one says, looking up with a beatific expression from a line of snap beans, "don't give us a quiz today." "Not today," laughs Will, and as we approach he and the student greet each other with an urban handshake—an elaborately choreographed series of claps, snaps, and finger rotations.

Will then leads me into the main entrance of the building and up the stairs to the English office. The walls of the school are covered with student artwork, bulletin boards announcing upcoming events, and framed art prints by Matisse, Picasso, and others. The floors and stairwells, I note, are remarkably clean, and Will reminds me that much of the maintenance in the school is done by students themselves, as part of the community service work required for graduation. "We've found," Will explains, "that when students are responsible for maintaining their own environment, they are more respectful of it; they seem to genuinely care for it more. No graffiti!" he says, spreading his arms out, "No trash." The school of 500 students manages quite easily with one janitor. "And the money goes right back into the school itself," Will says, "in the form of teachers. Last year we hired a local writer to teach a section of fiction writing with the money saved from our janitorial line."

One of the most striking features of Clifton High is the comfortable diversity that is manifest both in the student body and among faculty. In the 1990s, Will explains, there was a good deal of white flight from urban schools like Clifton. In the last decade, however, as schools successfully transformed themselves into teacher-centered institutions, professional parents were returning to public education in Cincinnati. Now Clifton boasts a rich diversity: The halls are filled with white, black, Asian, and Hispanic students, and the faculty seems almost as varied in their ethnicity: "It's amazing to think that fifteen years ago Clifton had only two African-American men on staff. In an urban school like this one, it's so important that faculty reflect the ethnic makeup of the student body. Everyone's got a positive role model here. Nobody's hanging out there alone."

The diversity of Clifton is also reflected in the impressive curricular and extracurricular offerings at the school. Many of the humanities courses have multicultural themes, and many of the after-school clubs demonstrate the great range of student interests and cultural backgrounds. There is a Latin dance club, and a Creole cooking club; a black arts club, and a Swahili club.

Will remembers his first six years at Clifton High School as both exhilarating and stressful. "I was observed a lot, and I learned a lot, too," he says. "There seemed to be a steady stream of classroom visitors—the chair, of course, and colleagues, but sometimes parents, too. Our school believes in an open door policy, and you could look up and there would be Adam Rosen's dad or Anna Pertzoff's mom. I once had a parent who audited my entire Russian literature class. She had better attendance than her daughter! I said to her, 'Crystal, I'll just give you my notes if you are so interested.' And she said, 'No, I want to learn this with the kids. I want to hear you speak.' And that was fine with me."

Will's first years were also complicated by graduate study. He knew that the district would require a master's degree for tenure, and he knew he needed to get started on it as soon as possible. The University of Cincinnati offered evening coursework toward a master's in English, and for two years Will drove there three days a week after school. These courses supplemented his intensive summer work at U. C. "The district paid 50 percent for the master's degree," Will explains, "but the work still had to be done 100 percent by me! And I really busted my ass in some of those classes. I took a Joyce seminar one summer—I'll never forget—we had to read all of Ulysses in four weeks." Will says the summer study had a great payoff. "I used to come back to my classes in the fall filled with renewed energy, like a spring wound up and ready to take off. All that intellectual work in the summer, all that talking about books and writing, it was bracing!"

Some of Will's saddest memories of his first years in the school involve the firing of friends and colleagues. "Tenure is hard to get. That's just a fact. And there were people—there still are—who were really nice individuals, really fine people, who just didn't teach well enough to stay. And you would say to yourself, 'Damn, this is really rotten. I can't believe they are letting this guy go,' but then another part of you would know the school was right, that this person was just not really great for the kids. It's always tough." Will still feels a particular sadness about the firing of his friend Adam, a fellow Swarthmore graduate who joined the school a year after he did. "Adam was brilliant, and one of the funniest people you'll ever meet. But the guy was lazy. Russ and Elizabeth and Paula were constantly on his back: Give more homework, vary your lessons, blah, blah, blah. But he was who he was and he couldn't change. They let him go in his fourth year, but it wasn't from lack of trying to keep him. They did what they could."

Will encountered some difficulties of his own during his first years at Clifton. "There were discipline problems in the beginning. As a rookie, I'd find myself in situation where I just didn't have a clue how to deal with certain kids." Will tells the story of a particularly troubled boy named Warren, with whom he had numerous confrontations. "The kid had problems, and because I was a young teacher, I tended to take his behavior personally; to see his actions as a kind of personal attack." Will says his colleagues in the English department were immensely helpful that year—sitting in on his class, modeling techniques and strategies. "It was, like, 'your problem is our problem; let's solve this together.'" When the boy got worse instead of better, the department backed Will in his appeal to have the child removed from the school and placed in the local alternative program. Will was also helped by the ample release time he was afforded for observing his mentor, Paula, in her own classes. "Any time I wanted to watch her—even on short notice—they found a way to cover my classes. And that's the way it has to happen: spur of the moment. You can't have a crisis and then be told, 'Okay, two weeks from Thursday you can watch your mentor teach.' It has to be then and there."

In the summer before his sixth year, Will spent two months scrupulously compiling the portfolio of his work that he would submit to the principal and the school board in the fall. In preparation, Will had saved over the years examples of his best materials: lesson plans and unit plans, creative assignments, and grading rubrics. He had samples of student work and research papers of his own that he'd written for his master's coursework. Reading through and organizing the six years' worth of labor gave Will a new perspective on his career. "I thought, wow, you really did do a lot of good work! I was really impressed with myself! It was a good feeling."

Will submitted the portfolio with an essay that synthesized his feelings about his growth as a teacher and his philosophy of education. "I felt when I wrote that essay that I really codified for myself what this teaching gig means to me. It was a good exercise to write that. And truthfully, by that point, I felt pretty confident that the tenure would work out. I knew what the administration thought of me. I knew what the parents thought of me. There was no mystery there." Will's portfolio sat in the principal's office, along with the portfolios of the three remaining teachers who had arrived with him six years before. A second copy had been submitted to the superintendent's office. Over the course of the fall, Will watched parents and veteran teachers leafing through his materials, and he knew the same thing was happening down at the central office. Will also knew that community members had been invited (via an article in the local paper) to write on his behalf (or against him) during this first few months of the year. By the time January came, Will was relieved that the process was over. "When I got that telephone call from Russ," he says, "my first thought was, 'Hallelujah!' My second thought was, 'Thank God that's over!'"

Will's tenure was greeted with real fanfare. He and his newly tenured colleagues were feted both at the school and at a special dinner given in their honor by the board of education. It was there that he first introduced his "work family" to his "real family" his fiancée, Janie, and her brother, Gene. "I remember thinking," says Will, "that I wanted everyone to like everyone else. I loved both sets of people, and I wanted them to get along. I knew they all were going to be with me for life."

With tenure came a sizable raise and with the raise came thoughts of home ownership. Will knew that he wanted to live right in Cincinnati—virtually all the teachers did—and he hoped to live close enough to even walk to school. "My neighborhood is not particularly lovely, in the traditional sense of the word," laughs Will, "God knows, there's some urban blight here. But how can I really understand the kids if I don't live near them? That's pretty much how everyone feels. And it didn't hurt that I got a low-interest loan from the feds to live here. Paying teachers to live near their schools is a great perk. It's great for us and its great for the kids."

Will found a modest three-bedroom house on King Street, just six blocks from the high school. In his seventh year, he made real a dream he had harbored since he was an undergraduate at Swarthmore: He set up a community reading group composed of parents and other neighborhood people. The group began as a slightly stilted teaching session, with himself as leader, but it gradually transformed into a true book group, where no one was teacher and no one was student. "Living in Cincinnati has transformed my views about what it means to be educated," says Will. "I came out of school something of a snob. I thought I had something to teach everyone. Living in this community has taught me how little I know. I've learned so much from the parents in my book group—about welding and refrigeration and how to make a dovetail joint; I've learned about how difficult it is to raise kids on one salary, and what kasha and varnishkas taste like. It's been an amazing learning experience."

As a tenured teacher, Will could now involve himself in the school in new ways. He had always considered himself something of a genius when it came to organization and structure. Russ had noticed his skill years before, when Will submitted to him, as part of a routine inventory, a color-coded chart of the English department book room, organizing the materials from most to least used, as well as by copyright dates and dates of purchase. Almost as soon as Will returned to school in his seventh year, Russ asked him to consider running for the scheduling committee—the faculty and administrative committee that establishes the yearly schedule for all teachers in the school. Will was glad to oblige. He knew that most of the work of scheduling was done on weekends and after school, but that he would be paid an extra $2,500 to do it. He relished both the money and the challenge, and he also thought, selfishly, that it would be good to have representation from the English department on the committee: He could ensure that his colleagues got decent schedules. "Getting on to that committee," Will says, "was really an important step for me. I realized once I started doing that work that I had a flair for administration. I really liked the camaraderie of working out this puzzle, this complicated schedule, with my colleagues. So then I thought, 'Hey, if you liked doing schedules, maybe you'd like doing curriculum.'"

Will ran next for the curriculum committee, and once again immersed himself in new curricular initiatives. Again he was compensated, and again he enjoyed the work. Will spent three Augusts poring over new curricular initiatives he found on the Internet and drafting materials to fit with his own department. Because the curriculum work was being done at the same time by representatives from the sciences and math departments as well, a natural inclination toward interdisciplinary study began to emerge: "I'm sitting there with Joe Sternbach and Carly Dachos, and we're talking about constructivist theory and the importance of narrative in math and science, and suddenly we see so many connections across disciplines. It just hit us in the face, and we started developing courses that cut across all our fields." By year eight, Will had created an interdisciplinary course that became a mainstay of the Clifton senior curriculum. The course, titled "What's Next?" combined cutting-edge science concepts with futurist theory, ethics, and science fiction. "It's a great course for seniors," Will explains. "They all see themselves on the brink of a brave new world. They love to imagine all kinds of doomed scenarios for the future and then figure out how to make things better." The school's curriculum committee has developed many other new courses over the years. "It's about the most creative work you can do," says Will. "I run for that committee whenever I'm eligible." Will figures that the curriculum committee alone saves the community the cost of two additional teachers' salaries. Five people work in the summer for $4,000 a piece. "That's less than a quarter of the salary of our former district curriculum coordinator for secondary instruction."

"When I first arrived at Clifton years ago," Will explains, "curriculum work was drudge work. Those were the dark days of high-stakes testing, and all of us teachers were held captive to those tests. I remember that morale could get really low. In March we'd say, 'You need to start drilling for this part of the test,' or 'You need to start pumping the kids full of this or that.'" Now standardized tests are used as one of many measures of student understanding. "The high-stakes testing almost ruined the profession," Will says. "Luckily, the state came to their senses. Otherwise, I would certainly not be here anymore."

After tenure, Will's responsibilities changed in other ways, as well. He mentored new teachers and did classroom observations of colleagues who were in their probationary period. Sometimes, too, he was called upon to observe and mentor those who were tenured. "Observations don't stop after you get your tenure here," Will explains. "We continue to have a policy of all-visitors-welcome. It's important not just for the school but for the teacher, too. You can't start feeling after tenure that you're all on your own. It's demoralizing, and it leads to burnout." In rare cases, tenured teachers have been asked to leave the school, and those cases remain vivid in Will's mind: "Given how well teachers are screened before they're hired and how rigorous our tenure process is, it's almost unheard of to let someone go after the seventh year. But it happens." Will tells a story of a teacher named Ann who started out at Clifton as a real star. She breezed through the tenure process and even won a state award for her innovative use of the computer in her classroom. But in her tenth year things had gone radically downhill. She stopped working altogether, sleepwalking through her classes; she stopped assigning homework and stopped grading the work that was turned in to her. Rumor had it that she was madly in love with a rock musician and that her many absences could be explained by the musician's touring schedule. Will and several other teachers had been called on to observe and advise their colleague, but their suggestions went unheeded, and the mild threats of the administration fell on deaf ears. "We had to fire her," Will says. "You can't have someone like that in the building. It ruins things for the other teachers.

But we documented our complaints and gave her every chance. She couldn't sue. She knew we were right. But the whole thing was really depressing."

More often, however, Will's out-of-class responsibilities are pleasant and even entertaining. "I've started a couple of clubs based on my own interests," he says. "I do a playwriting club every other year. We work with parents and put on the production the kids have written. It's great fun." This year, along with a new teacher in the school, Will established an Italian club: "This new guy, Ben, didn't get tenure in another district but he's working out great for us. He's fluent in Italian—which we don't offer in our school—so he teaches us the language, and we cook big Italian dinners with the kids on Fridays after school. Everyone's yelling 'Mangia! Mangia!' Then Janie and my two children come by, and we all eat. It's very pleasant."

It is fifth period, the last period of the day, and Will is teaching a sleepy class of seniors an elective he designed with the school guidance counselor titled "The Literature of Madness." It is late spring; the smell of mown grass and the sounds of a Frisbee game drift up through the open windows. The class is reading Nathaniel Hawthorne's story "The Birthmark," about a doctor whose maniacal obsession with perfection leads him to inadvertently murder his patient-wife. "Okay," he says, "let's look at some of the ways Hawthorne leads us to suspect the motives of the doctor. Where is the very first place in the story that you begin to wonder if Aylmer's priorities may be skewed?" There is much idle shuffling of pages. Mrs. Freeman, the mother of a bright transfer student named Sarah, raises her hand. "Yes, Mrs. Freeman," Will says, slightly dismayed that the first comment is not coming from a regular student. "As a wife myself," says Mrs. Freeman, "I have to be a little suspect of the line on the first page where it says that his love of his wife could only exist if it were entwined with his love of science. I think the wife should be number one; the career number two." Will can see Mrs. Freeman's daughter, Sarah, tuck her head down and smirk. He smiles. "What do the rest of you think?" he asks. "Family, one; career, two?"

"I agree with Sarah's mom," says Owen Daniels, a tall boy in the first row. "But I see this as something bigger than a tradeoff between career and family. It's a cautionary tale; like, too much interest in technology, not enough in people, leads to disaster." "Right!" Paul Corliss calls out from the back of the room. Paul had been something of a handful at the start of the year—his parents were going through a divorce and Will had to ask him to leave the room three times in the first months of school. After the third time, he had not been allowed back to Will's class until his parents signed him up for counseling. With the help of the counselor, however, he had settled in and was now a strong addition to the group: "This is just what we're talking about in my medical ethics class!" Paul says. "At what point does science interfere with humanity? Do we hurt a few people to help a lot of people?"

A heated discussion ensues, moving back and forth between the Hawthorne story, the medical ethics class (taught by the vice principal), and a series of news stories on stem cell technology and using animals in research. When the bell rings, no one leaves his seat. "Nature permits us to mar," Will reads from his book, "but seldom to mend." I'd like you to write two or three paragraphs tonight on Hawthorne's words on page 210. Pull together the ideas we talked about today, but go back more closely to the text." Everyone is jotting the assignment down in their notebooks.

After class I ask Will about the good discipline that is apparent in his classroom and in all the classrooms I pass in the school. "It's not that we have a zero tolerance policy; we don't. Some kids need more tolerance than others. It's just that if you have good curriculum and talented teachers and an administration that sends out the message of respect for the teachers, it's surprising how few discipline problems you get. If I decide I've got to send a kid out of the room for misbehavior, I know beyond a doubt that I'm going to be supported down at the office. No one is going to question my judgment. No administrator is going to say, 'You should have dealt with this yourself.' That kind of pro-teacher policy sends a powerful message to everyone in the building. It's such a relief, and it makes teaching so much easier."

At Clifton, students who are chronically disruptive are removed from the school and placed, either temporarily or permanently, in one of the city's alternative schools that are designed specifically for students who cannot work in the regular school setting. Specially staffed with clinicians and experts in child counseling, the schools have shown great success in securing high school diplomas for their students. Within Clifton stiff penalties exist for uncivil behavior. Students who curse and disturb the peace are fined seventy-five dollars. After a few tickets get written in September, you never again hear loud cursing in the hall. Students who damage school property are not allowed to return to the school until that property has been replaced. The strong emphasis on accountability has produced a peaceful and civil environment that is immediately apparent to any visitor.

Will takes me down to the faculty cafeteria, where several of his colleagues are eating an early lunch. The food at Clifton, Will says, is surprisingly good, partly because of a special fund from a local food distributing company that provides teachers with fresh salads and gourmet breads each day. The tables are covered with white tablecloths, and there is a vase of carnations and daffodils on the counter, next to a large coffee urn. A student, one of Will's second-period sophomores, comes to the table to refill his coffee mug. "I hope you're not planning to poison us," Will says to the girl, who grins back at us in a crooked hairnet. "You, Mr. Dewey? Not until I get my letter of recommendation from you for college!" Will lets out a hoot and bites into his grinder. Will explains that students can choose to work in the cafeteria to satisfy their community service requirement. "You'd be surprised how many kids elect to cook and serve here," he says. "Kids want to be useful. They just need to be given opportunities to help out."

After lunch Will walks with me to the parking lot outside Clifton High. It is the end of our two days of interviews, and I ask him if there is anything he may have forgotten to tell me. He stands in silent thought for a while, as the sounds of the school chorus rise up in the distance. "You know," he says, "it's hard to believe there was a time when young people didn't want to teach, when people thought about this as a profession of last resort. I've spent my entire career in this school and I feel like the luckiest guy in the world. I love my colleagues, and I love the kids. I'm not a rock star, I'm not a professional athlete, but I'm honored for the meaningful work I do, and I can't imagine anything better. My son says he wants to be a teacher. For a parent, I've got to say, that's a dream come true."

Bibliography

American Federation of Teachers, AFL-CIO. *Survey & Analysis of Teacher Salary Trends 2000*. http://www.aft.org/research.

American Institute of Architects. "Good Enough for Congress? A Pictorial Representation of Why Americans Deserve Better School Buildings." http://www.e-architect.com/gov/schoolpics.

Antonucci, Mark. "Tribute for a Light: Public Education Spending and Staffing." Education Intelligence Agency, May 2001. http://members.aol.com/educintel/eia/ tribute/table9.pdf.

Barone, Diane, ed. *The National Board Certification Handbook: Support and Stories from Teachers and Candidates*. York, Me.: Stenhouse Publishing, 2002.

Berliner, David C., and Bruce J Biddle. *The Manufactured Crisis: Myth, Fraud, and the Attack on America's Public Schools*. Reading, Mass.: Addison-Wesley, 1995.

Boaz, David. *CATO Handbook for Congress: 105th Congress*. Washington, D.C.: Cato Institute, 2000. http://www.cato.org/pubs/handbook/hb105-11.html.

Carpenter, Mark. "Education Not Litigation: The Paul D. Coverdell Teacher Liability Protection Act of 2001." Citizens for a Sound Economy, Capitol Comment 293, 21 March 2001. http://www.cse.org/informed/issues_template.php/590.htm.

Carter, Susan. "Incentives and Rewards to Teaching." In *American Teachers: Histories of a Profession at Work*, edited by Donald Warren. New York: Macmillan, 1989.

Cohen, R. M. "Schools Our Teachers Deserve: A Proposal for Teacher-Centered Schools." *Phi Delta Kappan* 83, no. 7 (March 2002).

Cohen, Rosetta and Samuel Scheer, eds. *The Work of Teachers in America: A Social History through Stories*. Mahwah, N. J.: Lawrence Erlbaum, 1997.

Coleman, James, et al. *Equality of Educational Opportunity*. Washington, D.C.: Government Printing Office, 1966.

Crosby, Brian. *The 100,00-Dollar-Teacher: A Teacher's Solution to America's Declining Public School System.* Sterling, Va.: Capital Books, 2002.

Darling-Hammond, Linda. *Doing What Matters Most: Investing in Quality Teaching.* New York: National Commission on Teaching and America's Future, 1997.

————. "How Teacher Education Matters." *Journal of Teacher Education* 51, no. 3 (May 2000).

————. "Professional Development for Teachers: Setting the Stage for Learning from Teaching." Santa Cruz, Calif., 1999. http://www.cftl .org/documents/Darling_Hammond_paper.pdf.

————. *The Right to Learn: A Blueprint for Creating Schools that Work.* San Francisco: Jossey-Bass, 1997.

————. "Teacher Quality and Student Achievement: A Review of State Policy Evidence." *Education Policy Analysis Archives* 8 (January 2000). http://epaa.asu/epaa/v8n1.

————. *What Matters Most: Teaching for America's Future.* Washington, D.C.: National Commission on Teaching and America's Future, 1996.

————. "Who Will Speak for the Children? How Teach for America Hurts Urban Schools and Students." *Phi Delta Kappan* 76, no. 1 (September 1994).

Darling-Hammond, Linda, and Barnett Berry. "Investing in Teaching: Doing What Matters Most for Student Learning." *Commentaries* 4, no. 3 (April 1998). http://www.nasbe.org/Educational_Issues/Briefs/ Policy_Updates/Teachers/doi ng.pdf.

Darling-Hammond, Linda, Arthur E. Wise, and Stephen P. Klein. *A License to Teach: Raising Standards for Teaching.* San Francisco: Jossey-Bass, 1999.

Education Week, "Quality Counts 2000: Who Should Teach? Policy Tables: Supporting New Teachers." http://www.edweek.org/sreports/ qc00/tables/ support-t1.htm.

Feistritzer, Emily C. *The Making of a Teacher: A Report on Teacher Preparation in the U.S.* Washington, D.C.: Center for Education Information, 1999.

Ferguson, Ronald F. "Can Schools Narrow the Black-White Test Score Gap?" In *The Black-White Test Score Gap,* edited by Christopher Jencks and Meredith Phillips. Washington, D.C.: Brookings Institution Press, 1998.

————. "Paying for Public Education: New Evidence of How and Why Money Matters." *Harvard Journal on Legislation* 28 (summer 1991).

Ferguson, Ronald F., and Helen F. Ladd. "How and Why Money Matters: An Analysis of an Alabama School." In Holding *Schools Accountable,* edited by Helen F. Ladd. Washington, D.C.: Brookings Institution, 1996.

Fetler, Mark. "High School Staff Characteristics and Mathematics Test Results." *Education Policy Analysis Archives* 7, no. 9 (26 March 1999). http://cpaa.asu.edu/epaa/v7n9.html.

Fideler, Elizabeth F., and David Haselkorn. *Learning the Ropes: Urban Teacher Induction Practices in the United States.* New York: Recruiting New Teachers, Inc., 1999.

Goldhaber, Dan D. "How Has Teacher Compensation Changed?" In *Selected Papers in School Finance.* Washington, D.C.: Urban Institute, 2000–01. http://nces.ed.gov/pubs2001/2001378_2.pdf.

Goorian, Brad. "Alternative Teacher Compensation." November 2000, Eric Digest 142, ERIC, ED 446368. http://eric.uoregon.edu/publications/digests/digest142.html.

Grant, Gerald. *The World We Created at Hamilton High.* Cambridge: Harvard University Press, 1988.

Gross, Martin L. *Conspiracy of Ignorance: The Failure of American Schools.* New York: HarperCollins, 1999.

Hammond, Ormond, and Denise Onikama. *At-Risk Teachers.* Pacific Resources for Education and Learning, 1997. http://www.prel.org/products/products/atrisk-teacher.pdf.

Hartocollis, Anemona. "Levy Says Higher Pay is Helping to Lure Teachers to New York." *New York Times,* 25 July 2002.

Hoffman, Nancy. *Woman's True Profession.* Old Westbury, N.Y.: Feminist Press, 1981.

Ingersoll, Richard M. "Teacher Turnover and Teacher Shortages: An Organizational Analysis." *American Educational Research Journal* 38, no. 3 (fall 2001).

Jencks, Christopher S. "The Coleman Report and the Conventional Wisdom." In *On Equality of Educational Opportunity,* edited by Frederick Mosteller and Daniel Patrick Moynihan. New York: Random House, 1972.

Jerald, Craig D., and Ulrich Boser. "Setting Policies for New Teachers." *Education Week* 19, no.18 (11 December 2000). http://www.edweek.org/sreports/qc00/templates/article.cfm?slug=policies.htm.

Jesness, Jerry. "Teacher Merit Pay." *Education Week,* 4 April 2001. http://www.edweek.org/ew/ewstory.cfm?slug = 29jesness.h20.

Johnson, Dale, and Bonnie Johnson. "The Unfairness of Uniformity." *Reading Today* (August/September 2002). http://www.reading.org/publications/rty/02aug_unfair.html.

Johnson, William. "Teachers and Teacher Training in the Twentieth Century." In *American Teachers: Histories of a Profession at Work,* edited by Donald Warren. New York: Macmillan, 1989.

Kozol, Jonathan. *Death at an Early Age: The Destruction of the Hearts and Minds of Negro Children in Their Boston Public Schools.* Boston: Houghton Mifflin, 1967.

Levine, Alan H., Eve Cary, and Diane Divosky. *The Rights of Students: The Basic ACLU Guide to a Student's Rights.* New York: Baron Books, 1974.

Ligon, Glyn D. "Data Quality: Earning the Confidence of Decision Makers." Paper presented at the annual meeting of the American Educational Research Association, New York, April 1996. http://www.educationadvisor.com/ocio2001/DATAQUAL.DOC_.

Liu, Edward, and others. "Barely Breaking Even: Incentives, Rewards, and the High Costs of Choosing to Teach." Harvard University School of Education, Cambridge, Mass., July 2000. http://www.gse.harvard.edu/~ngt/Barely%20Breaking%20Even%200700.pdf.

Lortie, Dan. *School Teacher: A Sociological Study.* Chicago: University of Chicago Press, 1977.

Lumsden, Linda. "Teacher Morale." March 1998, Eric Digest 120, ERIC, ED 422601.

Mann, Horace. *Annual Report of the Board of Education, Together with the Annual Reports of the Secretary of the Board, 1847–1852.* Washington, D.C.: National Education Association, 1947–1952.

Mehlman, Natalia. "My Brief Teaching Career." *New York Times,* 24 June 2002.

Monk, David H. "Subject Matter Preparation of Secondary Mathematics and Science Teachers and Student Achievement." *Economics of Education Review* 13, no. 2 (1994): 125–45.

National Center for Home Education, Issue Alert, 12 January 2000. http://nche.hslda.org.

National Commission on Excellence in Education. *A Nation at Risk: The Imperative for Educational Reform: A Report to the Nation and the Secretary.* Washington, D.C.: G. P. O., 1983.

National Council on Teacher Quality. *Teacher Quality Bulletin* 3, no. 3 (17 July 2002). http://www.nctq.org/bulletin/v3n3.html.

National Education Association. "Modernizing Our Schools: What Will It Cost?" June 2000. http://www.nea.org/lac/modern/modrpt.pdf.

National Humanities Alliance, Testimony on the FY2002 Appropriations for the National Endowments of the Humanities. http://www.nhalliance.org.

National Science Education Standards. http://www.nap.edu/reading room/books/nses/html/3.html.

Natriello, Gary, and Karen Zumwalt. "Challenges to an Alternative Route to Teacher Certification." In *The Changing Context of Teaching,* edited by Ann Lieberman. Chicago: Chicago University Press, 1992.

Nelson, F. Howard. *International Comparison of Teacher Salaries and Conditions of Employment.* American Federation of Teachers, December 1994. http://www.aft.org/research/reports/internl.htm.

Odden, Allan. "*Cincinnati's Teacher Evaluation and Compensation System.*" The Consortium for Policy Research in Education, University of Wisconsin-Madison, November 15, 2000.

Odden, Allan, and Carolyn Kelley. *Paying Teachers for What They Know and Do: New and Smarter Compensation Strategies to Improve Schools.* Thousand Oaks, Calif.: Corwin Press, 1997.

Okana, Kaori, and Montonori Tsuchiya. *Education in Contemporary Japan: Inequality and Diversity.* Singapore: Cambridge University Press, 1999.

Olson, Lynn. "Finding and Keeping Competent Teachers." *Education Week,* 17 July 2001. http://www.edweek.org.

Osgood, Charles. "Teachers in Residence." ACF Newsource, July 2001. http://www.acfnewsource.org/education/teachers_residence.

Perie, Marianne, and David Baker. "Job Satisfaction Among America's Teachers: Effects of Workplace Condition, Background Characteristics, and Teacher Compensation." National Center for Educational Statistics. http://nces.ed.gov/pubs97/97471.pdf.

Ravitch, Diane. "What Do Teenagers Want?" *Forbes Magazine,* 22 October 1997.

Reich, Robert B. "Standards for What?" *Education Week,* 20 June 2001. http://www.edweek.org/ew/ewstory.cfm?slug=41reich.h20.

Sack, Joetta L. "Schools Grapple with Reality of Ambitious Law." *Education Week,* 6 December 2000. http://www.edweek.org/ew/ewstory.cfm?slug=14idea.h20.

Scott, Willis. "Creating a Knowledge Base for Teaching." *Educational Leadership* 59, no. 6 (March 2002): 4–12.

Shanker, Albert. "The End of the Traditional Model of Schooling and a Proposal for Using Incentives to Restructure Our Public Schools." *Phi Delta Kappan* 71, no. 5 (January 1990): 345–57.

Shulman, Lee. "Knowledge and Teaching: Foundations of the New Reform." *Harvard Educational Review* 57, no. 1 (February 1987): 1–22.

Steinhauer, Jennifer. "Looking at Test Scores a Little Less Testily." *New York Times*, 2 August 2002.

Stigler, James W., and James Hiebert. *The Teaching Gap: Best Ideas from the World's Teachers for Improving Education*. New York: Free Press, 1999.

Trower, Cathy A. "Can Colleges Competitively Recruit Faculty without the Prospect of Tenure?" In *The Questions of Tenure*, edited by Richard P. Chait. Cambridge: Harvard University Press, 2002.

Tyack, David. *The One Best System: A History of Urban Education*. Cambridge: Harvard University Press, 1974.

U.S. Department of Education. *Digest of Education Statistics*, Washington, D.C., 1999. http://nces.ed.gov/pubs2000/digest99/.

———. *Digest of Education Statistics*, Washington, D.C., 2000. http://nces.ed.gov/pubs2000/digest00/.

———. *The Educational System in Japan: Case Study Findings 1998*. http://www.ed.gov/pubs/JapanCaseStudy/.

———. *Meeting the Highly Qualified Teachers Challenge: The Secretary's Annual Report on Teacher Quality*. Washington, D.C.: Office of Postsecondary Education, 2002.

———. National Center for Education Statistics. htttp://nces.ed.gov/fastfacts/display.asp?id-64; http:/nces.ed.gov/fastfacts/display.asp?id-96; http://nces.ed.gov/edstats/.

U. S. National Commission on Excellence in Education. *A Nation at Risk: The Imperative for Educational Reform: A Report to the Nation and the Secretary*. Washington, D.C.: Government Printing Office, 1983.

Viadero, Debra. "Teachers Seek Better Working Conditions." *Education Week*, 9 July 2002. http://edweek.org/ew/newstory.cfm?slug=16pay.h21.

Waller, Willard. *The Sociology of Teaching*. New York: Wiley, 1932.

Walsey, Patricia A., and others. *Small Schools, Great Strides: A Study of*

New Small Schools in Chicago. New York: Bank Street School of Education, 2000. http:/www.Bankstreet.edu/html/news/SmallSchools.pdf.

Weaver, Diane Dunne. "Are Small Schools Better?" *Education World,* 20 July 2000. http://www.education-world.com/a_issues/issues108 .shtml.

Weis, Eileen Mary, and Stephen Gary Weis. "New Directions in Teacher Evaluation." Eric Digest, December 2000, ERIC, ED 429052. http:// www.ed.gov/databases/ERIC_Digests/ed429052.html.

Winter, Greg. "More Schools Rely on Tests, but Study Raises Doubts," *New York Times,* 28 December 2002.

accountability, 92, 98, 113
administrators: evaluating teach-
    ers, 79, 83, 84, 89; interactions
    with teachers, 2, 19; managing
    student behavior, 47; misuse of
    power, 8, 19, 22; organizing
    professional development, 93;
    recruitment of new teachers,
    66, 68; teaching in the class-
    room, 30, 31; working with
    new teachers, 71, 93
Advanced Placement (AP), 38, 66,
    74
AFL-CIO, 115
alternative certification, 11, 61,
    63, 69
America Civil Liberties Union
    (ACLU), 43
American defense, education and,
    59
American Federation of Teachers,
    13, 15, 20, 22, 32, 95, 98, 115

Bloomberg, Michael, vii–viii
bonuses, 33, 96
Bush, George, 2, 28
business and education, 15, 17, 39

California, public schools and, 60
career ladder, 73, 86, 96

certification, 69; importance of,
    65
Chicago, small schools and, 53
class size 51, 59, 60
classroom environment, 46
Clinton, William Jefferson, 2
cognitive science, 62, 63
Coleman Report, 13
collegiality, 5, 23–24, 54, 87
computers, 50
Connecticut, certification and, 81
Consortium for Policy Research
    in Education, 20
consultants: teachers as, 54; out-
    side consultants, 91–92
cooperative learning, 5, 71
criminal activity, 45, 46
criteria for successful teaching,
    79, 84, 85

Darling-Hammond, Linda, 13, 35,
    60, 74, 75, 97, 116
department chairs, 30, 85, 101
Dewey, John, 1, 100
discipline: problems with, 40–46;
    proposals for change, 46–48
diversity, importance of, 70,
    104–105

Educational Testing Service
    (ETS), 21

English as a Second Language (ESL), 64
Essential Schools Movement, viii
Europe, teaching support in, 9
evaluation, teacher, 12, 23, 74, 81, 85, 96, 98

faculty lounges, ix, 50
first-year teachers, 71, 73
Freneau, Phillip, 7

Grant, Gerald, 41
guidance counselors, 29, 53, 111

Harvard University, 78
high-stakes testing, 97, 110
homeland security, education and, 59
housing incentives, 10, 27, 34, 70

in-service training, 12, 65, 91–92
Interstate New Teacher Assess-
    ment and Support Consortium
    (INTASC), 21
Irving, Washington, 7

James, William, 100
Japanese education system, 9–10, 14
Jefferson, Thomas, 6, 50

learning disabilities, 55, 63
Locke, John, 100
Lortie, Dan, 41

Mann, Horace, 8
master teachers, 21, 86, 87, 101
math, foreign-born teachers of, 70
math test scores, 60

mentoring, 11, 12, 71–73, 88–89, 102
merit pay, 21, 33
Mill, John Stuart, 100

A Nation at Risk (1983), 59, 74
National Board Certification, 22, 84
National Board of Professional
    Teaching Standards (NBPTS), 84–85
National Council for Teachers of
    Math (NCTM), 67
National Council for Teachers of
    Science (NCTE), 84
National Education Association
    (NEA), 26, 98
National Endowment for the
    Humanities (NEH), 94
new teachers, vii, 2, 11, 24, 27, 60–62, 70–75, 79–80, 83, 85, 88, 102, 116
New York City public schools, vii–viii, 60–61

Ohio, alternative certification and, 21, 101

paperwork, 28, 45
parents, 37, 43, 39, 41, 48, 51, 52;
    involvement in tenure deci-
    sions, 82–83
peer review, 95, 98
permanent certification, 81
Plato, 63
principals, 28, 30, 43, 47, 53, 55, 79
privacy, lack of, 39
private schools, 11, 50, 84, 93

psychologists, 45, 54
public education, 46, 69, 104

race, 18
recruiting new teachers, 11, 23,
    61, 63–69, 71, 73
respect, need for, 47, 62, 64, 74,
    87, 92–93
Rickover, Hyman, 59
Rousseau, Jean-Jacques, 63, 100

salary: bonuses, 22, 96; funding
    salaries in a teacher-centered
    school, 27–31; history of,
    16–20; poor compensation,
    15–16; proposal for changes in
    teacher compensation, 20–22
school environment: cleanliness,
    50, 51, 52; discipline problems,
    40–41; lack of civility, 39–40;
    proposal for improvement,
    46–51; work load, 38–39;
    working conditions, 4, 12, 18,
    37, 54, 64, 77, 94
school funding, 27–31; history of,
    50
school governance, 87–96
school reform, viii, 1–2, 7, 18
school violence, 2, 5, 40, 45, 56
science, teachers of, 69, 70, 78,
    84, 109
second-career individuals, 68–69
secretaries, 28, 29
Shakespeare, William, 101
Shanker, Albert, 15, 32
small schools, importance of,
    52–54
Smith College, 73
Social Security and teachers: gov-
    ernment pension offset law, 26;

Windfall Elimination Provi-
    sion, 26
special education 53
standardized tests, 20, 21, 82, 110
stipends: for administrative and
    curriculum work, 24; for sum-
    mer study, 94
student rights, 42–44
student teachers, 61
Swarthmore College, 99, 100

Teach for America, 26
teacher attrition, 2, 6, 11
teacher burnout, 6, 27, 34, 96, 110
teacher compensation: for passing
    National Board for Professional
    Teaching Standards (NBPTS)
    test, 22; knowledge- and skills-
    based pay, 21; merit-based sys-
    tems of, 21; pay for perform-
    ance, 20
teacher education programs, viii,
    11, 28, 62, 64, 65, 92, 100
teacher internships, 5, 69, 100;
    importance of, 64
teacher morale, 28, 29, 33–34, 37,
    38, 52–54, 87
teacher observations, 79–80, 85,
    89, 93, 110
teacher portfolio assessment, 80,
    82–83, 83, 89, 106, 107
teacher quality, 13, 31, 34, 59, 60
teacher testing, 65
teacher training, 11, 14, 32, 59,
    62, 71, 92
teacher unions, 8, 9, 15, 18, 22,
    24, 55, 56, 77
teaching: history of the profession
    6–9; lack of respect, 47, 62, 64,

74, 87, 92–93; poor status and
conditions, 1–3; stress and 44;
workload and, 38–39
tenure: cost efficiency, 79; necessity of, 77–78; proposals for
reform 79–86; teacher involvement in tenure decisions, 89
Texas: career ladder and, 81; merit
pay and, 21
textbooks, shortages of, 97
Title II Program, 28
Trumbull, John, 7

United Federation of Teachers
(UFT), vii

U.S. Department of Education, 10,
13, 35, 75

veteran teachers: as administrators, 87; as designers of curriculum, 90, 100; as mentors, 88;
importance of, 5, 6, 23, 71, 78;
sabbaticals and, 94

Wcingartcn, Randi, vii
wisdom of practice, 73, 86
working conditions, 4, 12, 47, 77;
importance for retention and
recruitment of teachers, 37, 64,
94; unions and, 18
workload, 38–39

About the Authors

Rosetta Marantz Cohen is a professor in the Department of Education and Child Study at Smith College. She began her career as a high school teacher in New York City. **Samuel Scheer** has taught high school English for twenty years. He has worked in Texas, New York, Massachusetts, and New Jersey. He is currently teaching at Windsor High School in Windsor, Connecticut.